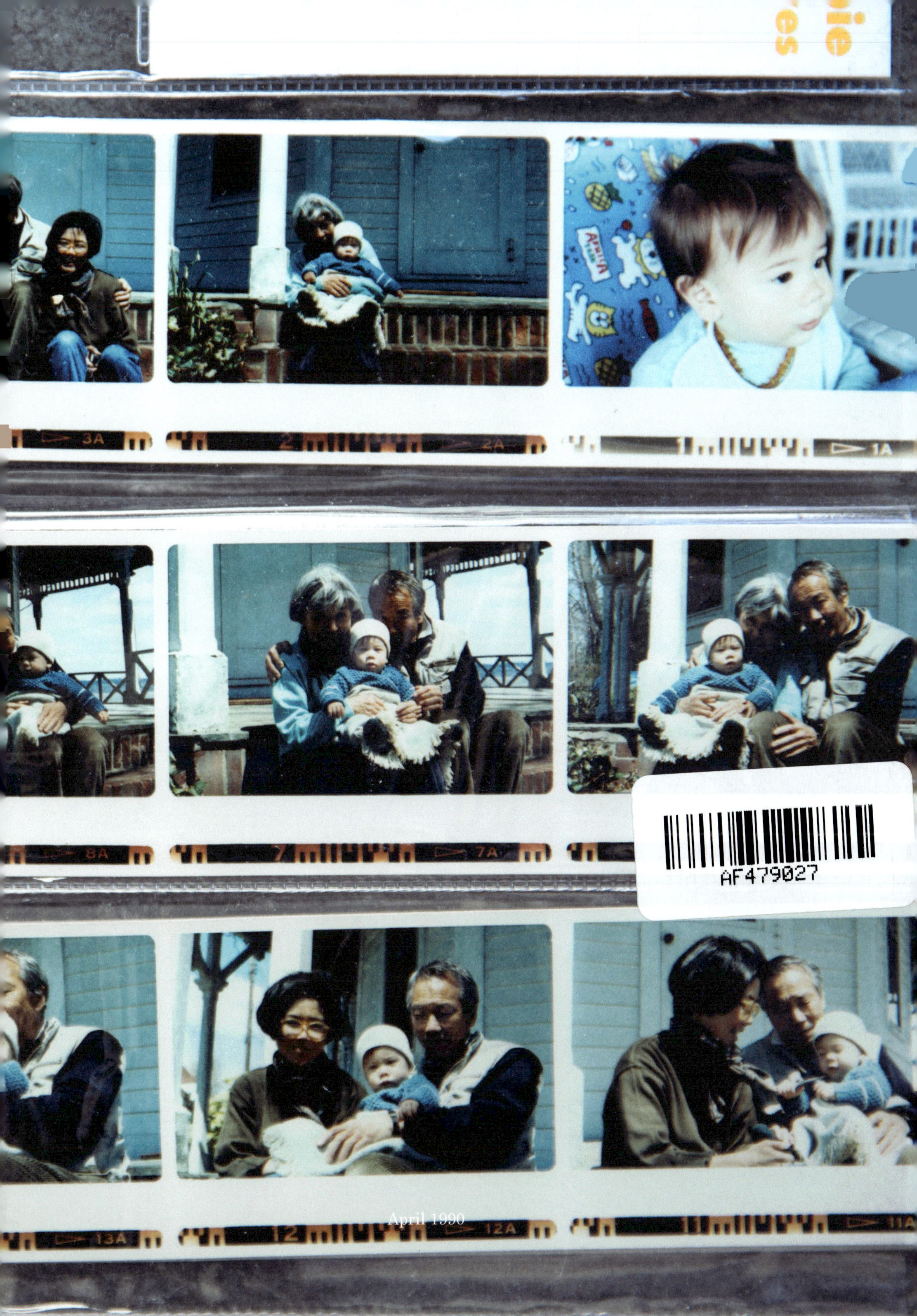
April 1990

Vulnerable Histories
(An Archive)

Koki Tanaka

Published by

Migros Museum für Gegenwartskunst
& JRP | Ringier

CONTENTS

Vulnerable Histories
Heike Munder

What happens when hate speaks? The violent rhetoric of hateful speech aiming to disparage and denigrate specific individuals or groups of persons has become a global phenomenon. More and more people, individually and collectively, are targeted by verbal assaults, which, like physical attacks, leave wounds. Language harbors the potential for such violation because we think of it as essential to what it means to be human. In speaking, we grasp the world around us by giving names to the objects in it, the American philosopher and philologist Judith Butler has argued, and so language is constitutive of who we are.[1] Yet when language is used to abuse rather than name someone, that person's identity and, by implication, his or her position in society are called in question. It is suddenly revealed that what the individual felt was a firm foothold in society is actually most precarious. The certainty of knowing who one is and where one belongs—a kind of self-assurance—gives way to a paralyzing sense of insecurity.[2]

The latest Amnesty International Report shows that social inequality and unfairness are on the rise around the world. Far from quelling this trend, the public statements of actors on the political stage add fuel to the fire. Minorities face growing defamation and demonization. Selected groups are purposely portrayed as existing outside the community; their

1   Language is not just the verbal utterance as such, it is also the performance of an action: by describing, we ascribe attributes, and so the mutual act of calling each other by names constructs human identity. A human being's self-conception is composed of the descriptions and designations given by his or her kin and the attributes ascribed by friends and acquaintances and, ultimately, society at large. By the same token, these attributes assign him or her a place in society and so instill in him or her a sense of community. See Judith Butler, *Excitable Speech: A Politics of the Performative* (New York: Routledge, 1997), 1–2, 5, 7–8.
2   See ibid., 4–13.

March 8, 2018

membership or exclusion is negotiated in a strident (verbal) discourse informed by discriminatory simplifications.[3] Examples include the slogans of right-wing parties across Europe such as the Alternative für Deutschland (AfD) in Germany, the Front National (FN) in France, the Freiheitliche Partei Österreichs (FPÖ), which is now part of the Austrian government, Hungary's Fidesz (Hungarian Civic Alliance), and Prawo i Sprawiedliwość (PiS, Law and Justice) in Poland; and, in the United States, the rhetoric of President Donald Trump and his team of advisors as well as the "alt-right" movement, which has grown in strength since Trump was elected. Racist resentments also poison relations between ethnic groups in Asia. The Chinese, for example, make no effort to integrate the African minority living in their midst, while in Japan, the ultra-nationalist group Zaitokukai organizes rallies at regular intervals to agitate against the *Zainichi*, the ethnic Koreans living in Japan.

These observations raise the pressing question of how societies can counteract xenophobia, nationalism, and populism and the associated decline of (humanist) values that is on display every day in ordinary interactions and the news media. How can we promote a shared community life based on tolerance? Understanding each other would seem to be essential if we hope to preserve and even cherish diversity. One way to prompt such dialogue is communal initiatives like those modeled in the actions of the Japanese artist Koki Tanaka (b. Tochigi, Japan, 1975). Since the 2011 Fukushima nuclear disaster, Tanaka's creative practice has increasingly focused on coexistence in societies and questions of participation and sympathy. The artist stages multiday workshops inspired by the observation that crises engender temporary new forms of community; the films and photographs documenting these events form his oeuvre. The actions unite people with very different backgrounds in the art context, where they explore the possibilities of cooperative action by taking on challenges arranged by the artist. What all his pieces have in common is that they lift the protagonists out of their daily routines; in their perspective, Tanaka's projects are an "exceptional situation" set in a microcosm unto itself. The scenarios he develops put the artist himself

3   See Amnesty International, ed., *Amnesty International Report 2017/2018: The State of the World's Human Rights* (London, 2018), 12–14.

March 8, 2018

in the role of sociological observer, transposing issues relevant to society into the art context. The assignments that effect this translation are ordinary and common tasks. For example, the participants in *Provisional Studies: Workshop #7 How to Live Together, and Sharing the Unknown*, a workshop he realized in the framework of the 2017 Skulptur Projekte Münster, were asked to cook a German dish from the time of World War II. Researching a recipe, shopping for the ingredients, and preparing the meal, they chatted about food that brought back childhood memories, which led them to talk about their lives and, more generally, the past and how to live with it.[4] In the context of Tanaka's workshop, exchanging personal histories is an ethical act; such specific moments in which understanding is created are exemplary, gesturing toward a universal insight: an active discourse is fundamental to tolerant coexistence. On the one hand, people discover that beneath the specifics of place and personal situations, their experiences, good and bad, are similar, enabling them to join in the search for solutions to (urgent) social and political issues. On the other hand, simply talking about problems and fears can help them understand each other better. The artist's workshops remind us that we should not remain silent when confronted with populist slogans and racist exclusion, however common they may be; we should acknowledge the explosive dynamic behind them and never flinch from discursive engagement. Tanaka's workshops offer one format of such engagement sheltered from the heat of political debates.

The project he has realized for his solo exhibition at the Migros Museum für Gegenwartskunst represents a thematic return to the artist's native country. A "returnee" himself—he lived in Los Angeles for a long time—he turns the spotlight on a highly sensitive subject: the resentments toward foreigners in Japan, which have grown steadily more widespread since 2009. The primary target of the nationalists' enmity is the ethnic Korean community, known as *Zainichi* (which means, simply, "resident in Japan"); its main sponsor is the anti-Korean organization Zainichi Tokken o Yurusanai Shimin no Kai (Association of Citizens against the Special Privileges of the Zainichi), or short Zaitokukai.

4 See Koki Tanaka, *How to Live Together: Production Notes. Produktionsnotizen* (Münster: Skulptur Projekte Münster, 2017), 8–9.

March 8, 2018

There are currently just under 500,000 Koreans living in Japan (out of a total population of 127 million, as of 2015).[5] The great majority of them are descendants of families that have lived in Japan for several generations; their ancestors came as—more or less voluntary—labor migrants during the Japanese colonial rule over Korea in the first half of the twentieth century (1910–1945). During the next few decades, they were subject to a restrictive policy of cultural assimilation: they were obliged to speak Japanese and assigned Japanese instead of their Korean names. After the end of Japanese colonial rule, many Koreans returned to their home country—those who stayed in Japan were now considered stateless. The long history of forced assimilation and marginalization has left a deep imprint on the relations between Koreans and Japanese. Yet the history behind the hostilities that have flared up with novel intensity in the twenty-first century goes back even further, to before the colonial period. One decisive event was the Great Kantō earthquake of 1923, after which mobs attacked Koreans living in Japan. In an essay included in the present volume titled "*Zainichi* Koreans and Racism in Japan," the *Zainichi* Korean sociologist Tong-hyon Han offers a detailed discussion of relations between Koreans and Japanese in the past and present.

The contemporary right-wing discourse denigrates the Koreans living in Japan as parasites in Japanese society and beneficiaries of a state that allegedly accords them preferential treatment.[6] These accusations raised by the ultranationalist groups are easily shown to be baseless, but that does not stop rabble-rousers from agitating, especially on the internet, where they vilify their victims as "vermin," tell them to go back to

5　　See Ministry of Justice Japan, ed., "Statistics on the Foreigners Registered in Japan," 2017, www.ipss.go.jp/p-info/e/psj2017/PSJ2017-10.xls (accessed March 7, 2018), and United Nations, Department of Economic and Social Affairs, Population Division, ed. "World Population Prospects. The 2017 Revision," https://esa.un.org/unpd/wpp/DataQuery/ (client-specific data requested through the website, accessed March 7, 2018).

6　　See The International Movement Against All Forms of Discrimination and Racism—Japan Committee, "Rise of Hate Speech in Japan," *Focus*, vol. 74 (December 2013), https://www.hurights.or.jp/archives/focus/section2/2013/12/rise-of-hate-speech-in-japan.html (accessed March 8, 2018).

March 8, 2018

Korea, and even threaten to kill them.[7] The Japanese government has been slow to respond to this development. A so-called "Hate Speech Act" was passed in 2016, yet it criminalizes not hate speech in general but only specific slogans, making it easy to circumvent the ban by changing the phrasing of verbal assaults.[8] Given the lack of an unambiguous legal definition of discrimination and an anti-discrimination law, the violent rhetoric targeted at the *Zainichi* continues unabated. The rallies often draw very few actual marchers and achieve their impact primarily online, where slogans, photographs, and videos circulate unchecked, establishing a permanent public presence that infests the collective consciousness. Racist propaganda shapes public opinion, leaving no room for historical realities and fact-based narratives. Demonizing generalizations crowd out any accurate portrayal of the people being attacked and their individual stories.

In his new workshop *Vulnerable Histories (A Road Movie)* and the documentary films of the same title, Koki Tanaka contrasts the Zaitokukai's propaganda with two personal histories. Loosely based on the motion picture *Before Sunrise* (1995), the plot revolves around two protagonists who first meet each other in Tokyo during the nine-day filming between March 28 and April 9, 2018. They are Woohi Chung, a *Zainichi* Korean woman, and Christian Hofer, a Swiss national whose Japanese great-grandparents emmigrated to the United States around the turn of the twentieth century. Various settings serve the two as points of departure for conversations in which they tell their individual stories and revisit the recollections of family members. Tanaka is interested in personal and conscious memories of specific situations, but also in the collective memory of communities, a subconscious stratum fed by the experiences of friends, relatives, and acquaintances. In the exchange

7   See "Hate Speech in Japan: Spin and Substance–A Troubling Rise in Xenophobic Vitriol," *The Economist*, September 24, 2014, https://www.economist.com/news/asia/ 21620252-troubling-rise-xenophobic-vitriol-spin-and-substance (accessed March 8, 2018).

8   See "A Year After Enactment of Hate Speech Law, Xenophobic Rallies Down by Nearly Half," *The Japan Times,* May 22, 2017, https://www.japantimes.co.jp/news/2017/05/22/ national/social-issues/year-enactment-hate-speech-law-xenophobic-rallies-nearly- half/#.WqEad62ouUk (accessed March 8, 2017).

March 8, 2018

between the protagonists, their (family) histories become the subject of the workshop, which is designed as a road movie. The title *Vulnerable Histories (A Road Movie)* points to the risk they incur when they open up to a stranger and share their personal lives: to trust someone is to be vulnerable. And it hints at a salient aspect of their narratives, which exemplify the lasting wounds dealt by experiences of exclusion and racist resentments across generations. Verbalizing these injuries can confer a kind of recognition that gives the lie to the Zaitokukai's defamatory slogans. As a form of working through history, the personal narratives are flanked by lectures by sociologists and historians who speak to the protagonists about the present-day situation and history of the Korean minority and the legal situation around hate speech in Japan. Also as part of the workshop, the protagonists review YouTube videos documenting racist marches and visit several historic sites such as the memorial commemorating the Korean massacre following the Great Kantō earthquake that are emblematic of the deep rift between Koreans and Japanese.

With the dialogue set in the microcosm of the workshop at its heart, Tanaka's work underscores that communication and discursive engagement are indispensable for a community life based on open-mindedness and tolerance. *Vulnerable Histories (A Road Movie)* undertakes a probing inquiry into the lack of mutual understanding and distrust that mar the coexistence of Japanese and Koreans. Tanaka points up that one should not acquiesce in the resulting social exclusion; it is not a "societal reality" to be accepted. Everyone is called upon to seek active community engagement: the appeal is locally specific in intent, but its implications are universal. All over the world, citizens need to be vigilant when it comes to racism, discrimination, and nationalism and untiring in their efforts to contribute to a community life in which everyone feels valued. Their most important tool, the artist suggests, is the lively discourse that can be initiated by even the smallest and most "commonplace" collaborative action. Where conversation leads to the discovery of shared experiences and builds acceptance for diversity, communities grounded in sympathy can come into being.

Tanaka's solo exhibition in Zurich will present the films in which he documented this project. A series of workshops to be held in the city

March 8, 2018

in conjunction with the presentation will use Tanaka's works as spring-boards for an exploration of questions concerning community, solidarity, tolerance, and social cohesion across the divisions of racism and national-ism. The exhibition is intended as a platform for dialogue, with the films providing vital impulses. The idea is to turn the museum into a site of active discursive involvement—a space that accommodates doubts and dissent so as to counteract the general tendency toward radicalism and polemics.

March 8, 2018

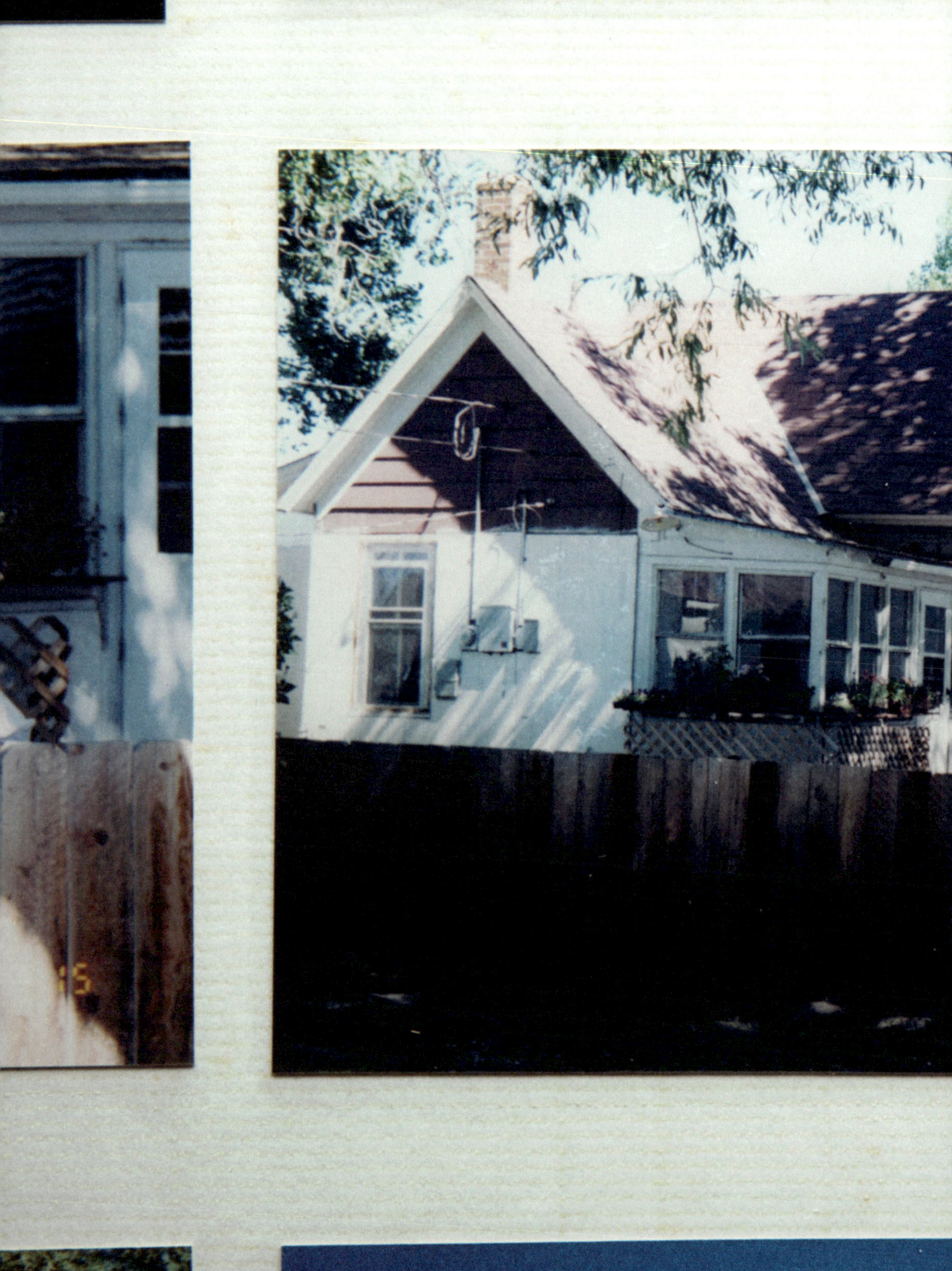

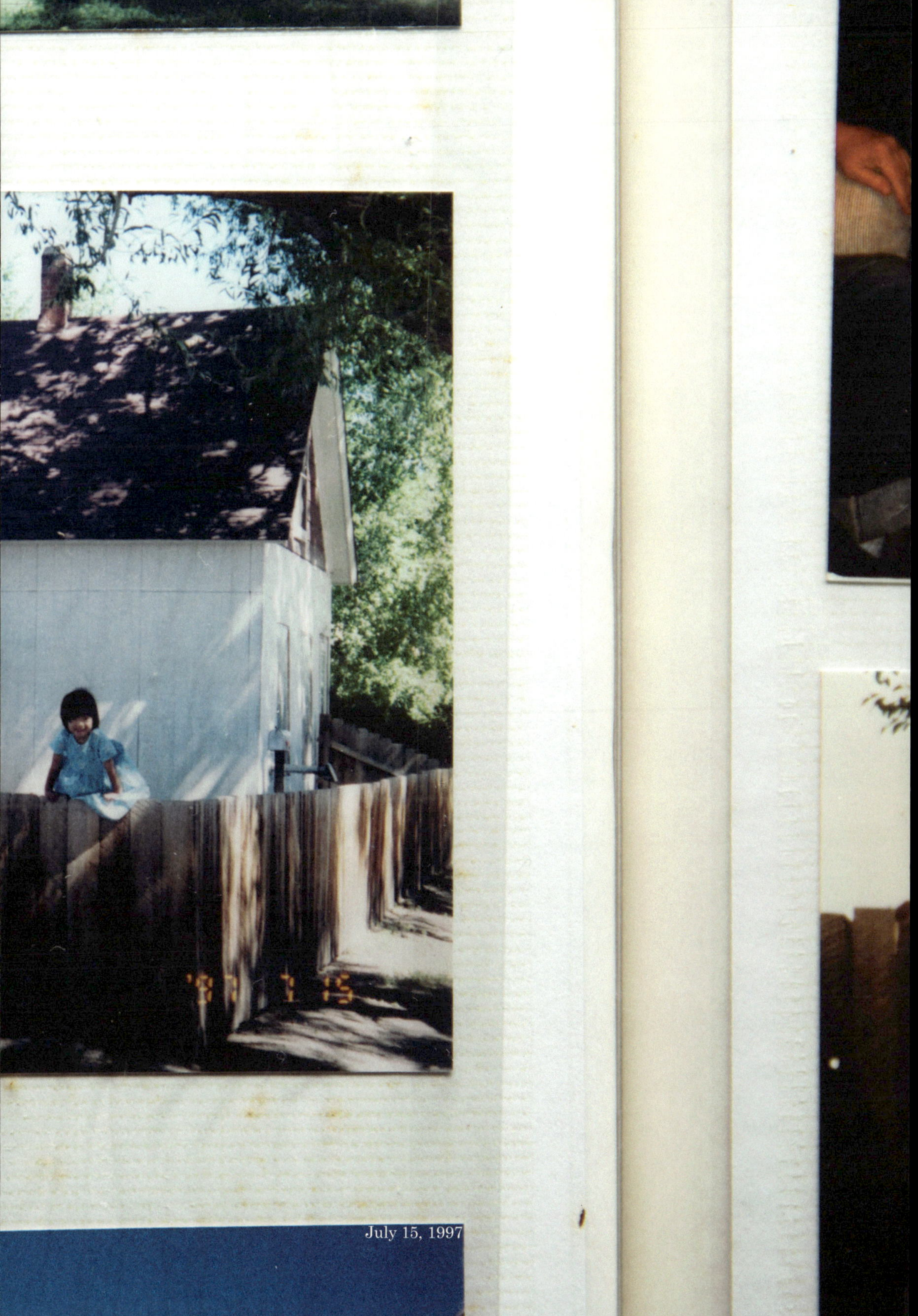

July 15, 1997

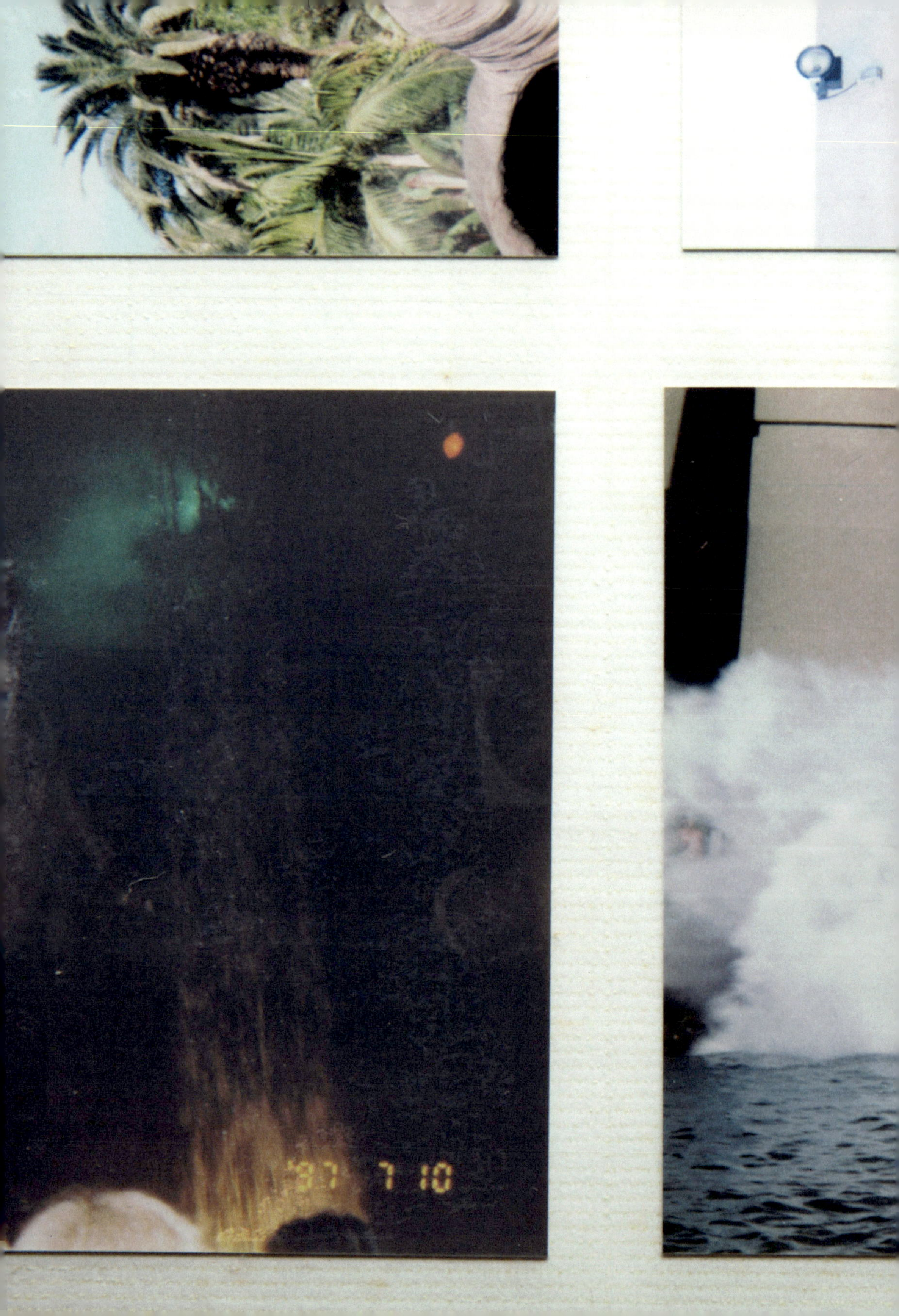
'97 7 10

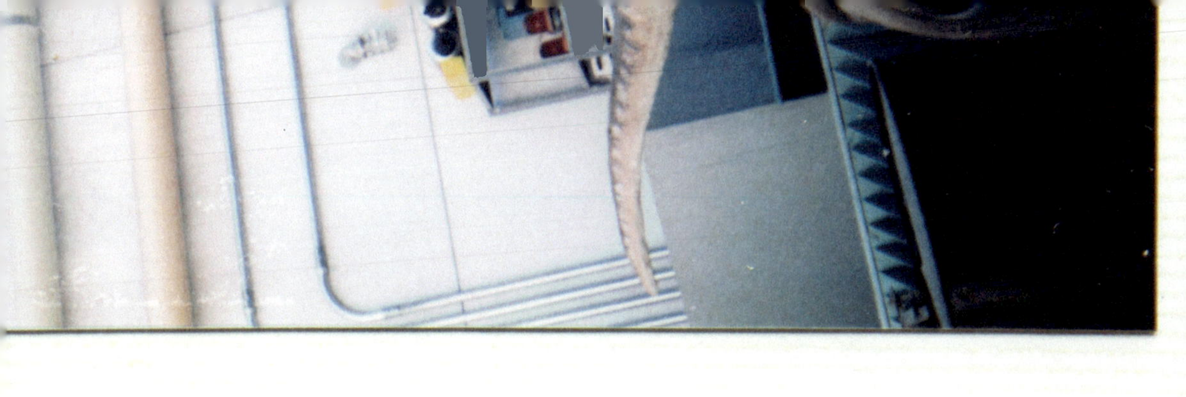

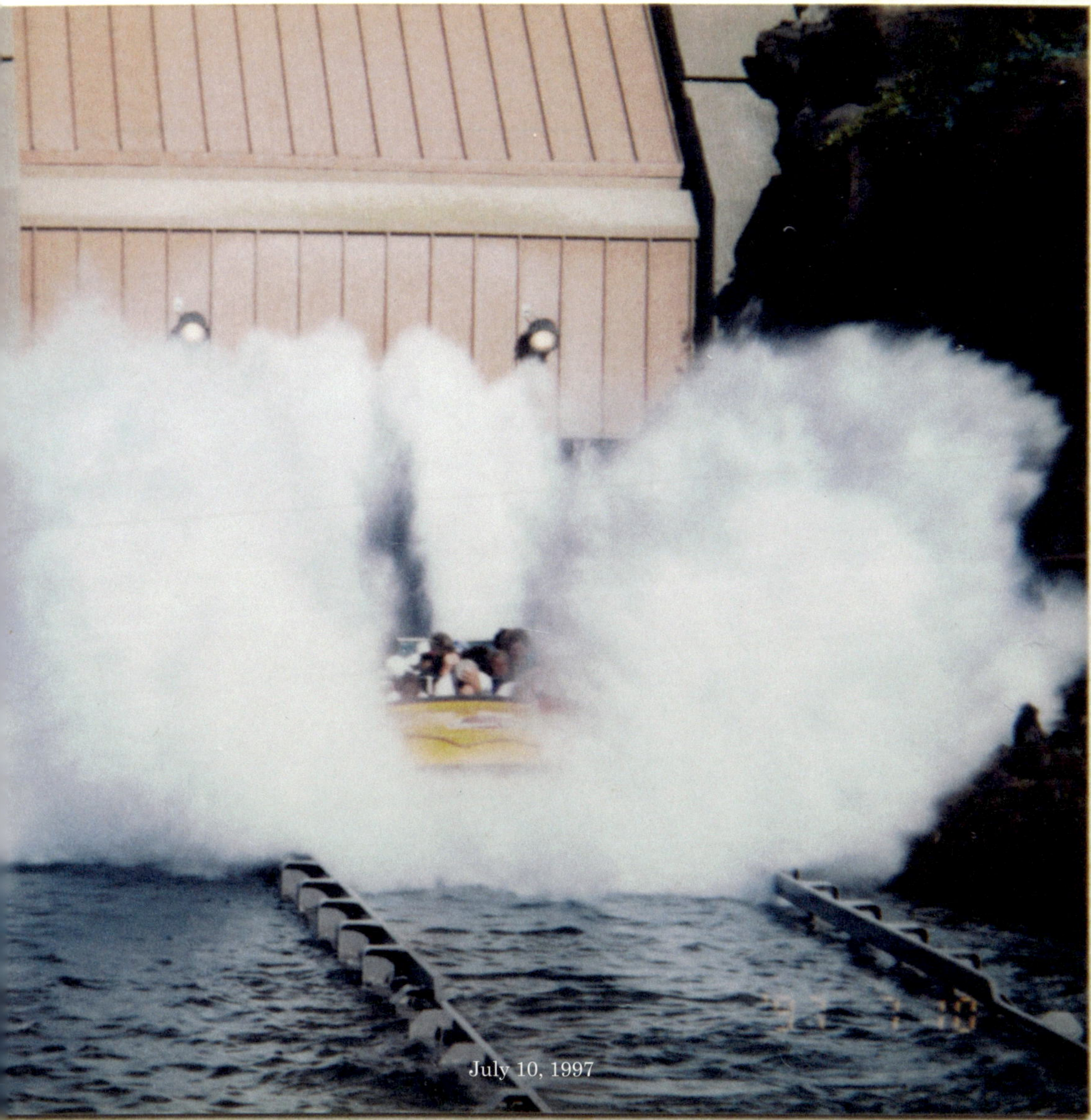

July 10, 1997

Reflective Notes
Koki Tanaka

About These Notes
I wrote these notes over the course of the film shoot. There were nine days of filming. Including the short break in between, I spent about two weeks in Tokyo working on the films.

April 11, 2018

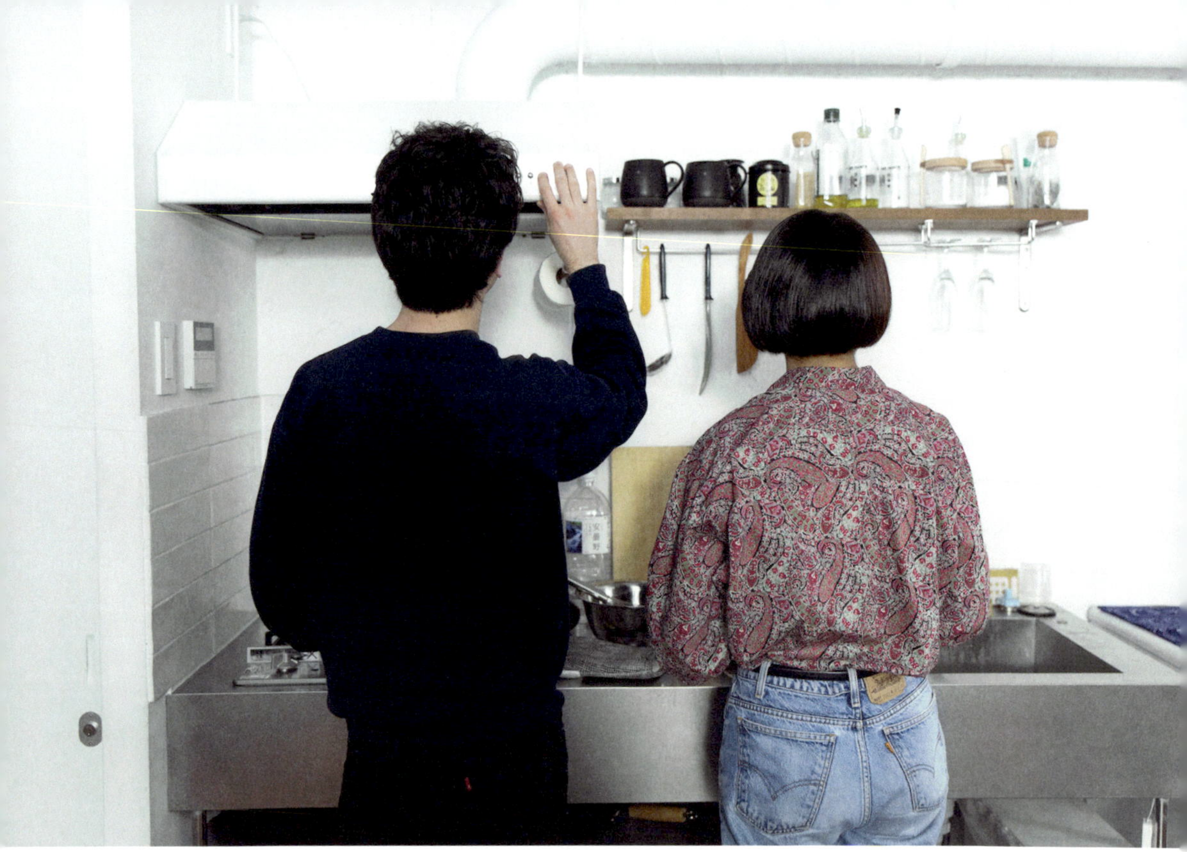

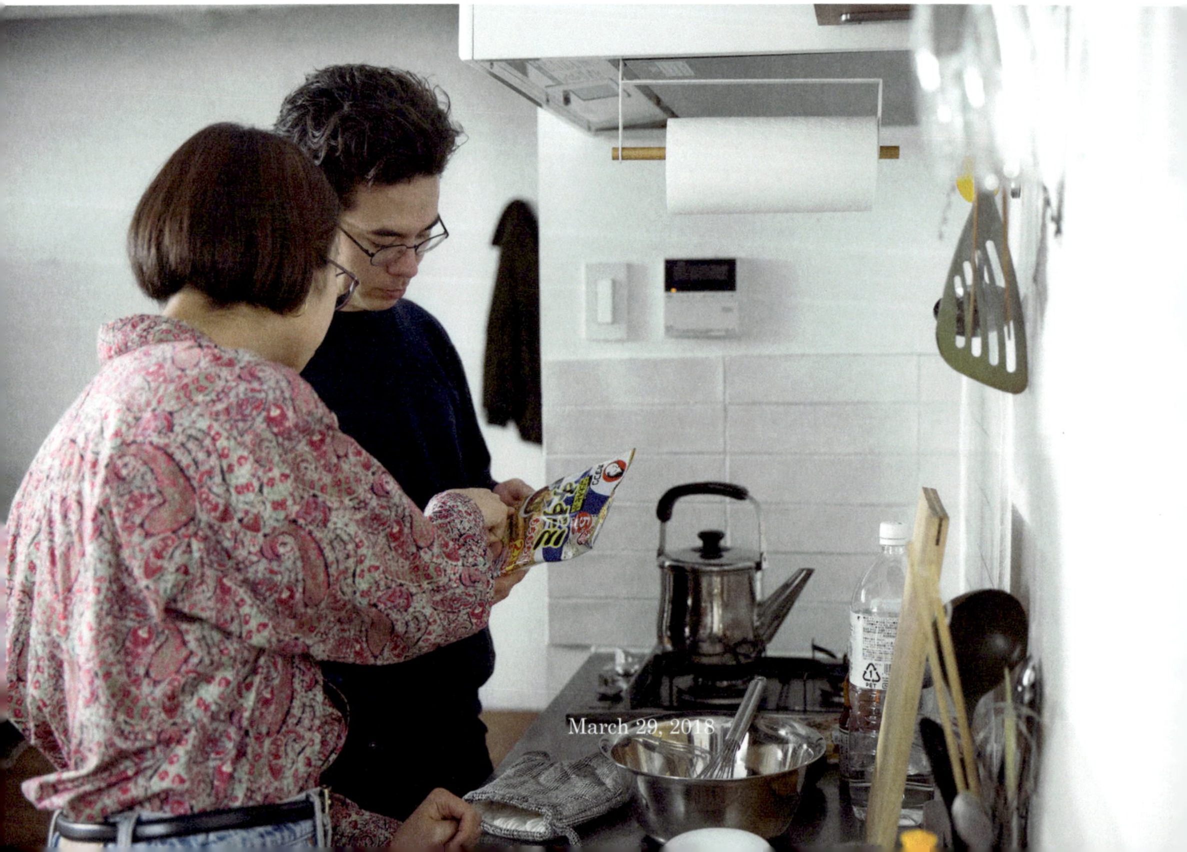

March 29, 2018

Thematic Thoughts on the Project (the First Brief)

Who can predict the situation that you see the issues around "xenophobia" and "racism" in media worldwide again and again? New kinds of racist movements by white supremacists in the United States after the Trump election, Islamophobia in Europe after terrorism by ISIS, as well as the "refugee crisis" related to the civil war in Syria. Closing borders by European countries is an instant reaction to the "refugee crisis," and Brexit is one of the results of denial against considering "how to live together."

Nationalism is a global phenomenon nowadays—in Japan too. One social problem is hate speech toward Korean residents of Japan (*Zainichi* Koreans), which emerged over the past decade. The issues around refugees and immigrants are entering a new phase in contemporary history.

Why can't we accept differences and find something common rather than hate someone different? I think each instance of racism has a local context and historical reference. But at the same time, I think there is a similar form that connects multiple problems across multiple places. And if you know the similarities that connect these problems, you can see the local problems differently. Therefore you can get a fresh perspective by comparing several problems—surveying several contexts to understand what is common as well as to get to know more about the domestic issues. This project is an attempt to obtain such a perspective for understanding multiple situations, and also to find out how we can understand each other.

The protagonist who comes from Europe meets another protagonist in Japan to form a pair who explore the situation in Japan regarding racism, anti-foreignism, and xenophobia. The films are both a sort of "road movie" in which the protagonists meet people and visit sites, and/ or a study trip that focuses on the emerging problem of "hate speech" toward *Zainichi* Koreans in comparison with the situations in Europe and the United States.

September 9, 2017

Two Letters

This project begins with two letters: one addressed from Woohi Chung to Christian Hofer, and the other from Christian Hofer to Woohi Chung (see pp. 73–87 of this volume). I asked Woohi and Christian to write about their families in letters to each other. I thought that writing about their families could offer them a way to explain their backgrounds. And it would also allow the public who read the letters to see where those family histories stand in relation to modern history.

What makes a letter a letter? A letter has an addressee. Each writes to the other. But they do so with the knowledge that their letters will also be read by other people. It is both intimate and public. In this project, the two will have to reveal their thoughts and emotions to the camera. Their letters are an introductory exercise for a project in which the private is made public.

April 3, 2018

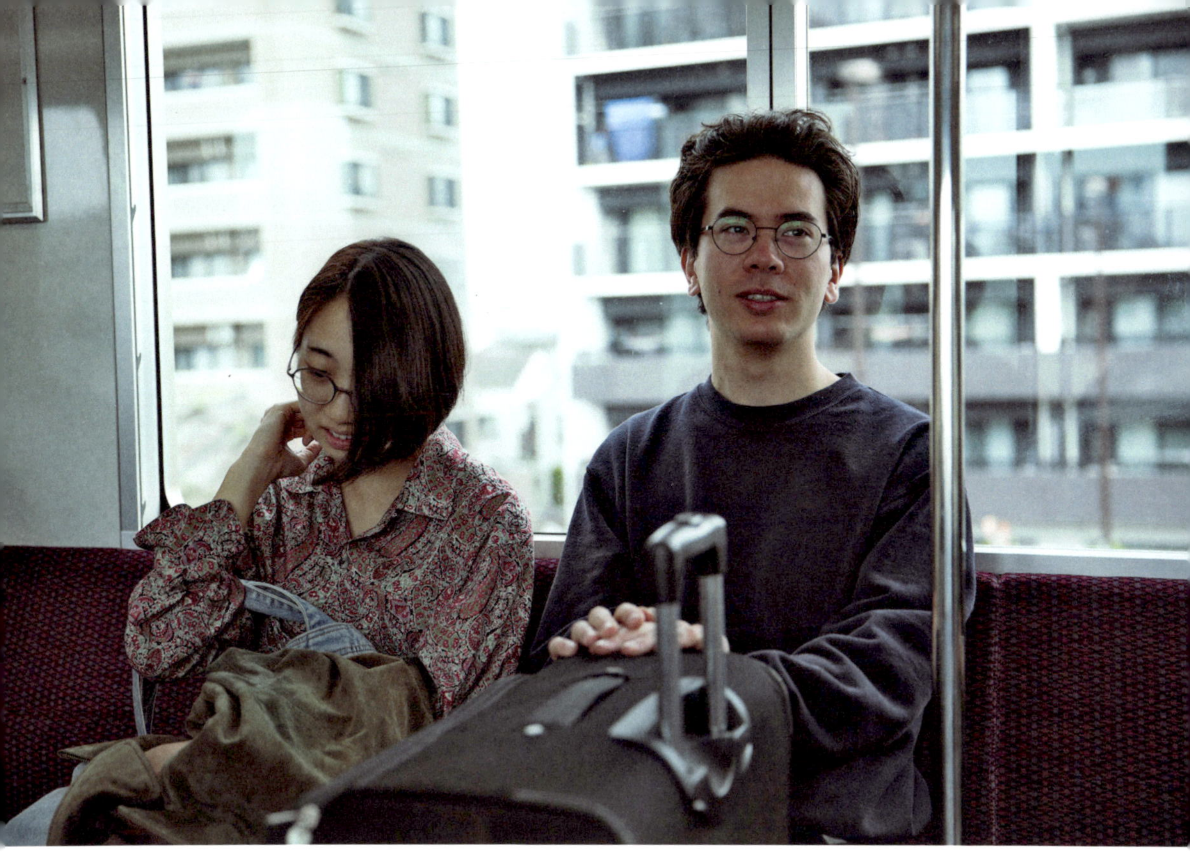

April 6, 2018

Directing from Continuity

In my projects so far, the approach has generally been to take a film crew to another country and then shoot with local participants/actors. But this time the filming will be done in Tokyo and its environs. Since I live in Kyoto now, it takes me several hours to get to Tokyo by high-speed rail—but it's still close enough that I can go anytime the need for a meeting arises.

So I have a sense that I've never really had before: a sense that the preparations and the meetings and the film shoot all flow seamlessly into a single continuity. I would almost say I have the sense that my life and the films are blurring into each other. I suppose this has also affected my approach to directing. Before, it was enough for me to set up the rules and the framework for filming the group dynamic. We would document the participants/actors as they moved freely about in the set up. Everything that was said/done there was left to chance. This time, I decided to hold as many meetings with the protagonists as possible, to talk with them about the topics I wanted them to talk about, and to have them share in my intent and vison. I wanted them to be creative collaborators, and not just subjects for observation.

TUESDAY, JANUARY 23

Preliminary Study Session for Cast and Crew

Producing a film entails gathering people with different skills to form a temporary team who will complete the project through their collaborative labor. The camera operator, the sound recordist, the production manager—the production is an assemblage of all their skills.

In the production process, the artist has the role of conceiving the overall concept and framework, and then whether it goes well or not depends on the artist's ability to share that vision with the film crew. Of course it's necessary to share practical details (including something as basic as whether to shoot mainly on tripods or to rely more on handheld cameras), but sharing the contents of the work is also important. And so this time I organized a preliminary study session for the cast and crew during preproduction.

At the study session I had the sociologist Tong-hyon Han, who also advised on the overall direction of this project, present an overview on the history of *Zainichi* Koreans and their current situation in Japan (the presentation was based on the text that is reprinted on pp. 101–108 of this volume), and then asked the sociologist Takahiro Akedo, who specializes in laws related to hate speech, to give a talk comparing hate speech regulations in Europe and the United States and the situation in Japan (this was connected to the selection of the laws that Woohi and Christian would be reading for the films).

Thinking that the Great Kantō earthquake that struck the Tokyo area in 1923 and the lynching of Koreans living in Japan that occurred in the earthquake's aftermath could serve as reference points, I also asked Tadahito Yamamoto, who is a curator at the Center of the Tokyo Raids and War Damage in Tokyo, to first guide our group on a private tour of the Memorial Hall and the Great Kantō Earthquake Memorial Museum in Yokoamicho Park, where there is also a memorial to the Korean victims of the disaster.

At the Great Kantō Earthquake Memorial Museum, we saw photographs, paintings, architectural models, and statistical graphics documenting both the devastation caused by the earthquake and the

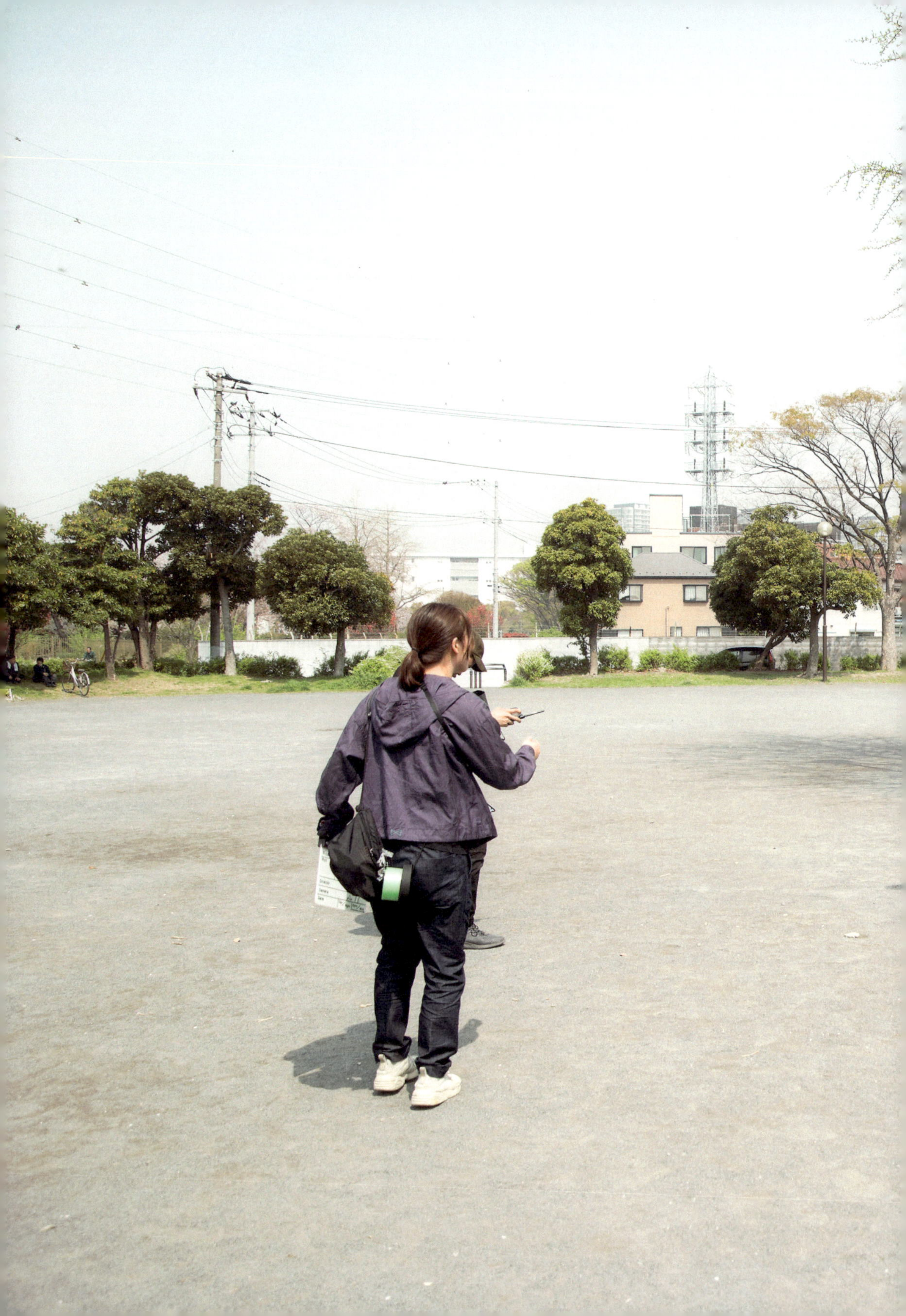

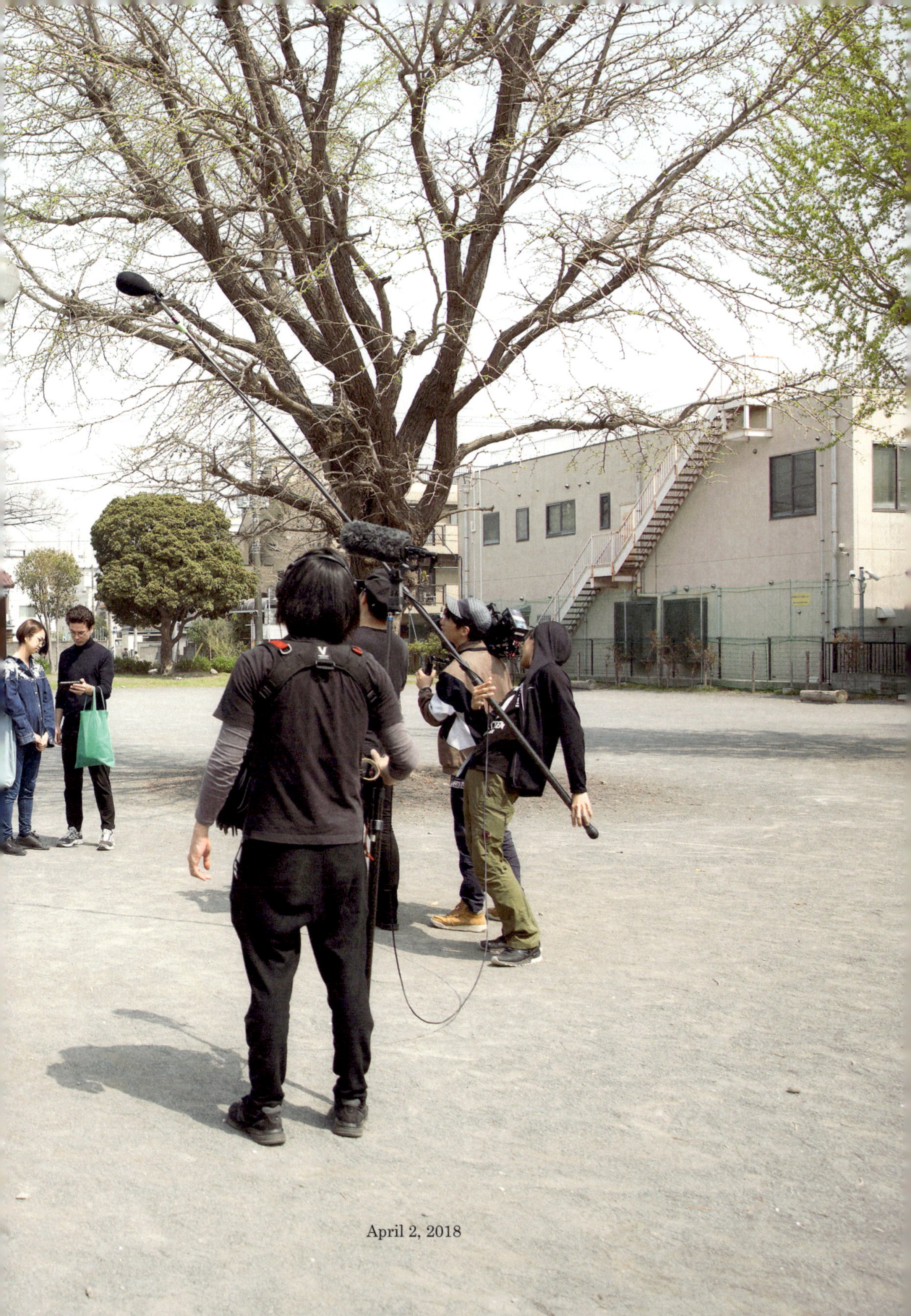

April 2, 2018

subsequent recovery efforts. Out of all these displays, Yamamoto paid particular attention to the many paintings that were hung in the Memorial Hall and in the museum. He said that it was possible to recognize in them the first signs of the development that led to the use of art for state propaganda during World War II—the so-called "war pictures" genre.

The memorial to Korean victims is placed outdoors in the park, somewhat removed from the Memorial Hall, and there is hardly any mention of the lynchings in the museum. Instead, documents of the American air raids on Tokyo during World War II are juxtaposed with the natural disaster of the earthquake. In treating the man-made tragedy of war as if it were equivalent to a natural disaster, the display in a sense obfuscates the question of war responsibility.

Yamamoto is a specialist in the Tokyo air raids, but I asked him to speak about the ambivalent politics of the planning and realization of the Great Kantō Earthquake Memorial Museum, where there is a contradiction embedded in the building between state power's vertical objective of focusing everything on the recovery of the imperial capital, and the horizontal diversity of the artifacts from the disaster that are on display, many of which were donated by private individuals.

April 3, 2018

FRIDAY, MARCH 29

 # Understanding and Exchanging Positions 1: Cooking
The first thing I have the participants/actors in my projects do is cook together. One reason is that it helps them to break the ice, but also, at a stage when the overall direction is still unclear, it provides a relatively achievable task as the first activity in getting started and preparing to spend the coming days together. Within the dynamics of several people cooking together, it is also a natural way of determining the roles that each participant/actor will play in the group.

But this time it has a slightly different significance. I had spoken with Woohi in advance about what to cook, and we decided upon making the Korean-style savory pancakes known as *chijimi* in Japanese. Woohi and Christian would cook the same *chijimi* that Woohi's mother makes at her *izakaya* (a Japanese pub)—which, instead of following the traditional recipe, is a fusion dish that includes avocado and shrimp. This project takes shape through Woohi communicating or even "teaching" what she knows about *Zainichi* Korean issues to Christian. In that sense, the cooking scene could be seen as a metaphor for the entire project.

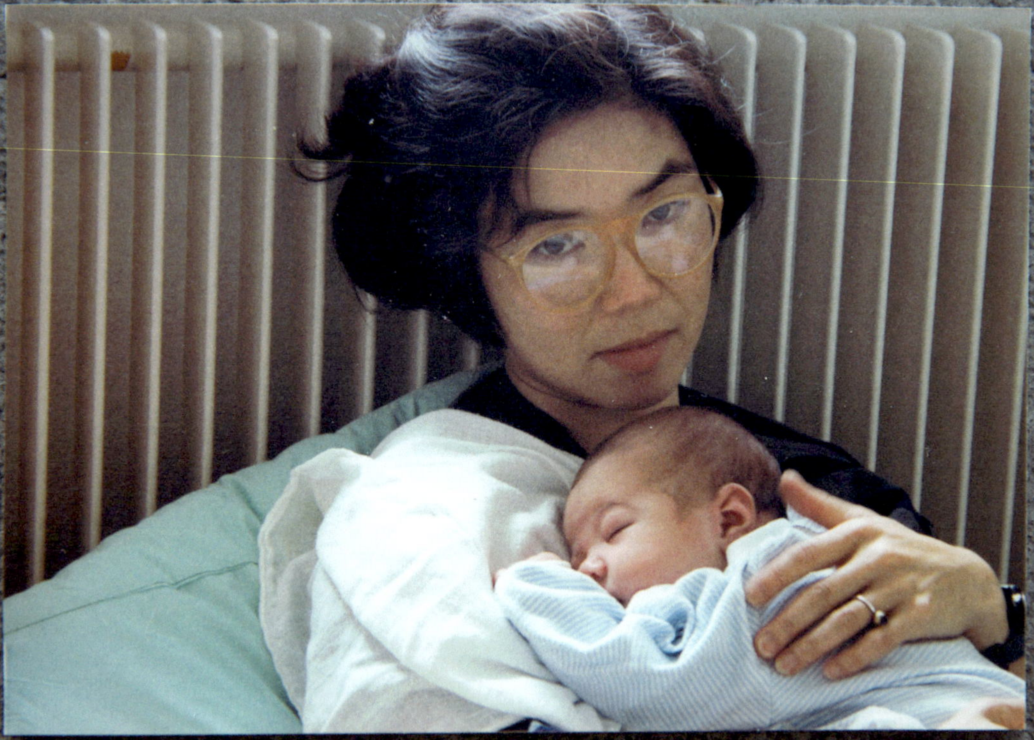

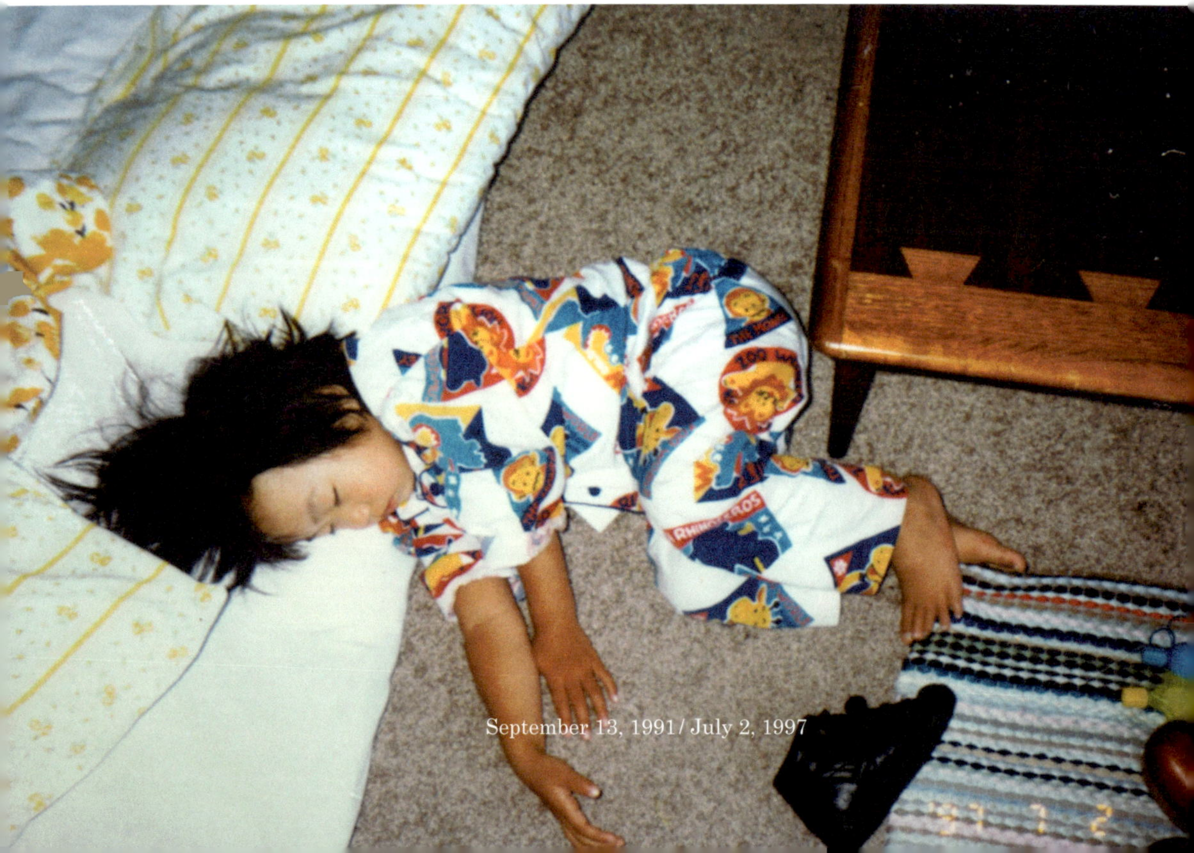

September 13, 1991/ July 2, 1997

Understanding and Exchanging Positions 2: Family Photographs
I asked Woohi and Christian to bring family photographs to share with each other. People still used film in the 1990s, and the materiality of the prints had a nostalgic feeling. Parents, grandparents, and other relatives made appearances as the pair flipped through their childhood photographs. Sometimes a building could be seen in the background, or a figure would be rendered entirely in shadow against the backlight.

As the photographs got older and older, the grandparents seemed to age in reverse. An image gradually formed of their experience as first- and second-generation *Zainichi* Koreans. What kind of childhood, and what kind of youth did Woohi's father and mother have? Or what about Christian's grandfather, who was incarcerated at the Manzanar concentration camp during World War II for being Japanese American—what did Japan mean for him, or the United States? Talking about the family photographs led to talking about the history of *Zainichi* Koreans in Japan, and the history of Japanese people in the United States.

April 3, 2018

Record / Focus / Voice: Filming Workshop

Woohi and Christian would be spending the entire film shoot surrounded by cameras and mics. Here, I wanted them to understand the basic elements of what it means to make a film.

1. The present recorded by the camera can be immediately played back as footage of the past. Film is a technique for capturing the constantly fleeting present in a document and replaying it over and over.
2. If the camera is out of focus, the world seen through its lens will be blurry and indistinct. The act of focusing on something in the frame is the same as deciding on what to pay attention to in reality.
3. Woohi and Christian would be wearing wireless mics throughout the film shoot. I thought they should be aware how sensitive the mics are—because to wear the mics is also in a sense to expose their bodies (voices) to the public.

April 11, 2018

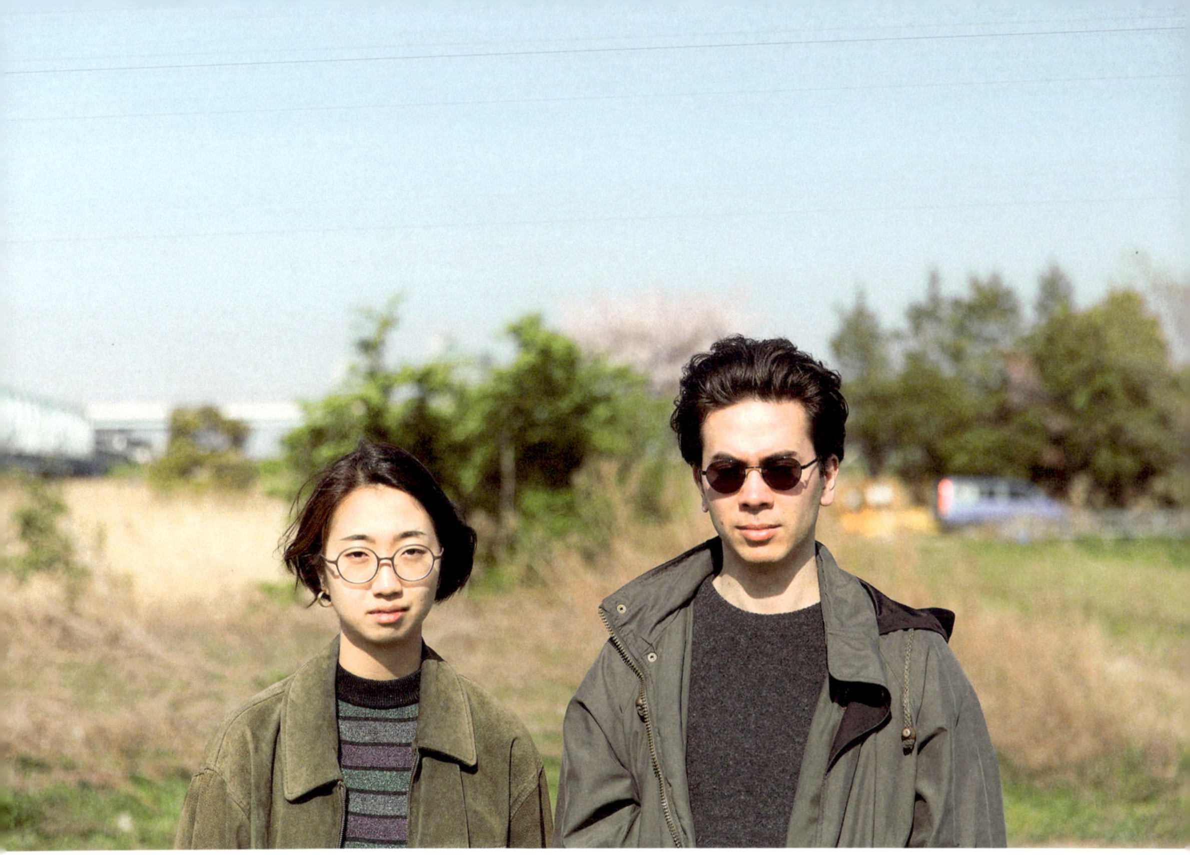

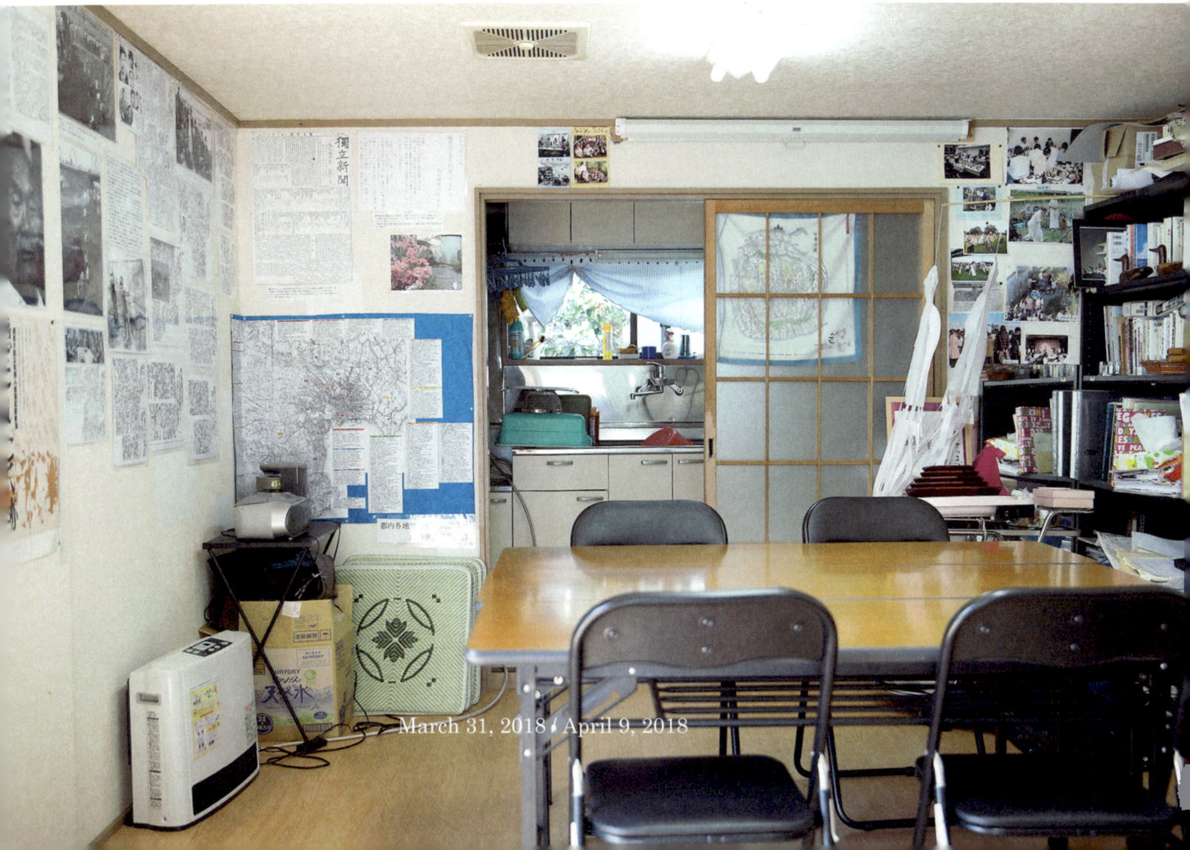

March 31, 2018 / April 9, 2018

SATURDAY, MARCH 31

 # History—Visiting a Site 1: Arakawa

On September 1, 1923, Tokyo and the surrounding region were struck by a massive earthquake (the Great Kantō earthquake). In the aftermath, there was a surge in demagogic attacks on Korean people. Claims that the Koreans had poisoned the wells or were using bombs to start fires spread through the populace in the form of rumor, or through unconfirmed reports on police radio, or through confused newspaper articles, leading to the lynching of Koreans by vigilante mobs and the military. Due to the ensuing cover-up, most of the victims were left unaccounted for, and their remains have never been found.

The area around the former Yotsugi Bridge on the Arakawa river is one of the few symbolic sites of this history, as extant documents and individual testimonies have established with relative certainty that killings took place there. The citizen's organization Housenka has erected a memorial to the victims nearby. In fact, the original plan was to place the memorial on the riverbed, where the killings actually took place and the dead bodies were piled, but the national authorities denied them permission. Later, the owner of an *izakaya* next to the river offered a plot for use, and the memorial was set up on private land.

Masao Nishizaki has been involved with the issue of the lynchings for over thirty years now, starting from when Housenka was established. The main activities of Housenka have been to collect oral histories, search for remains, and erect the memorial, but over time the organization has become a kind of community center for the neighborhood, and a place where people gather.

April 3, 2018

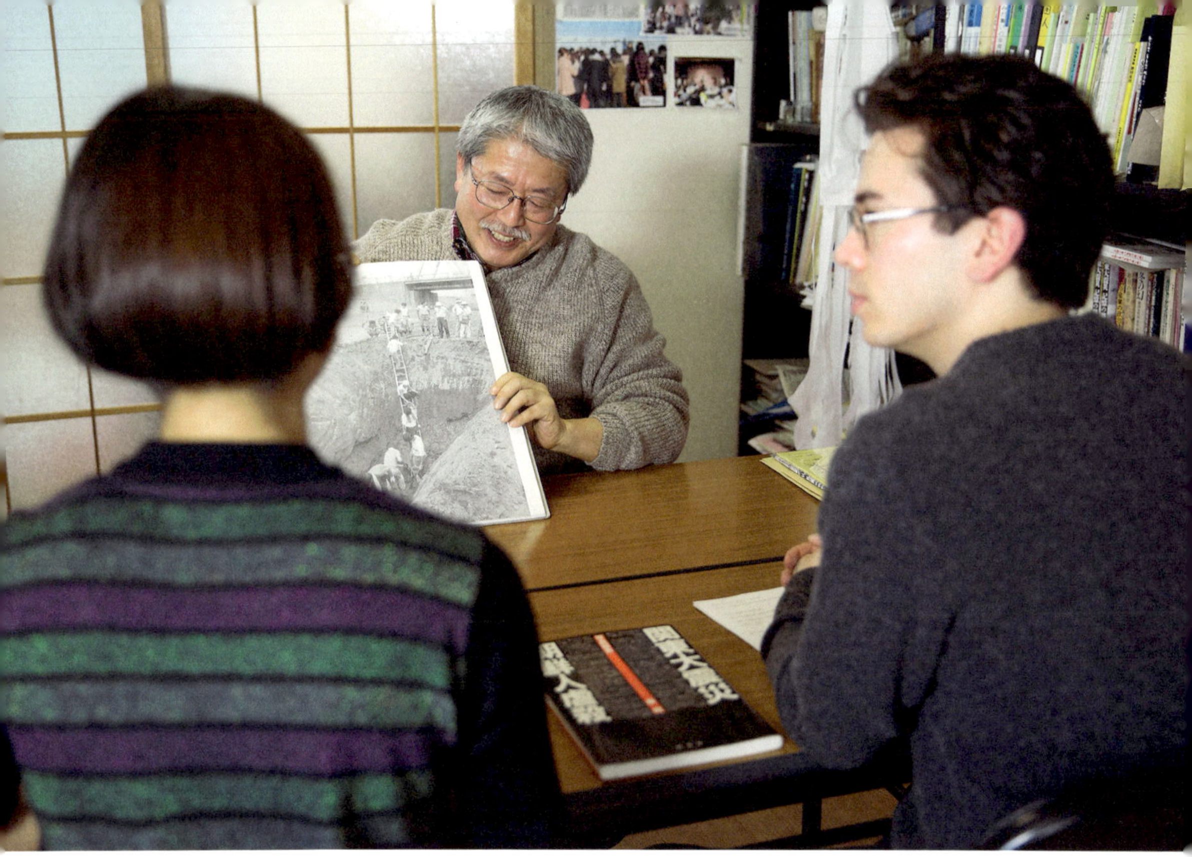

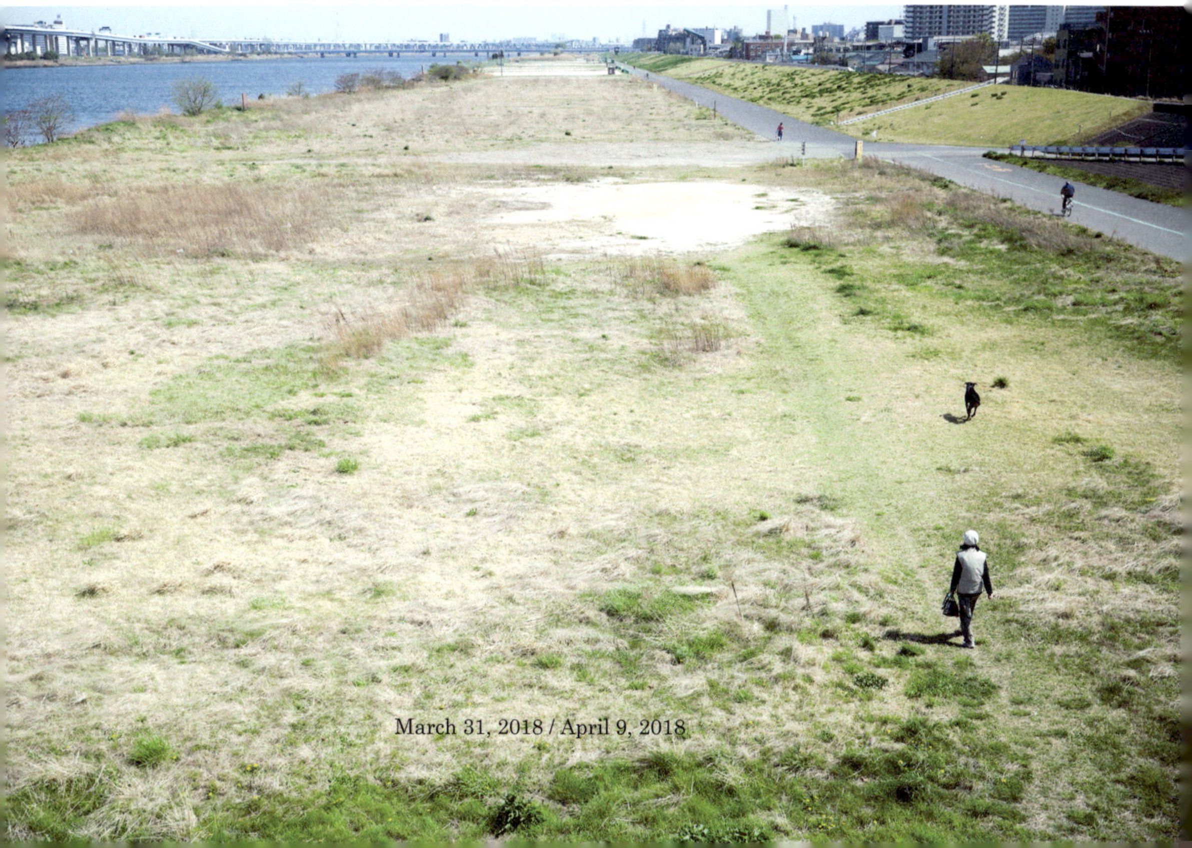

March 31, 2018 / April 9, 2018

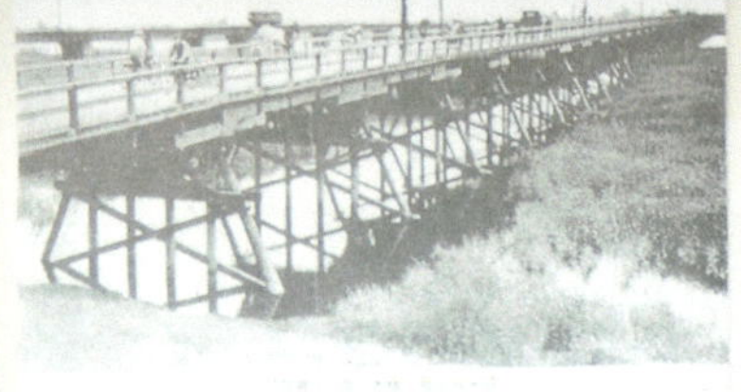

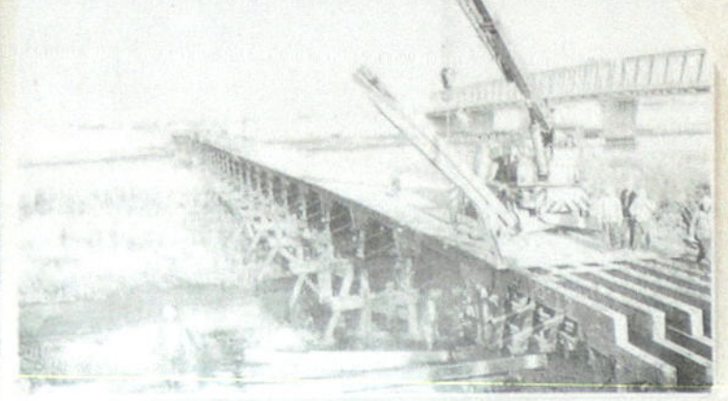

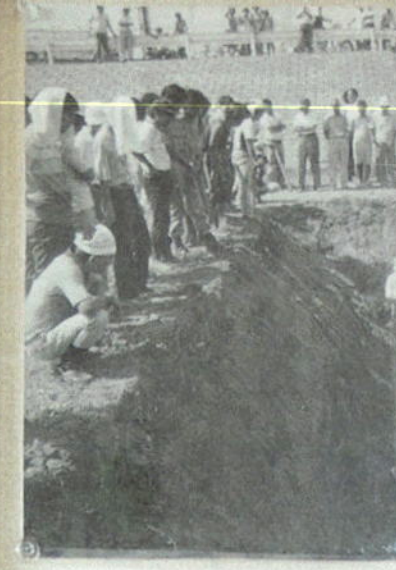

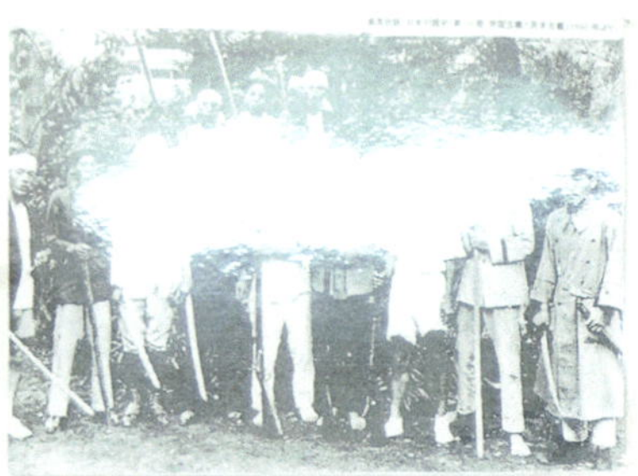

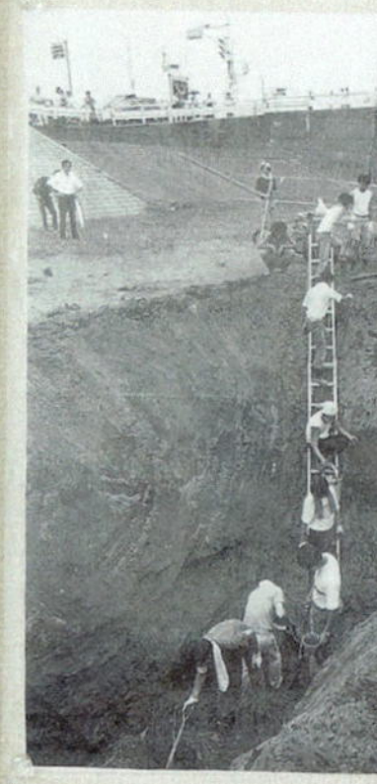

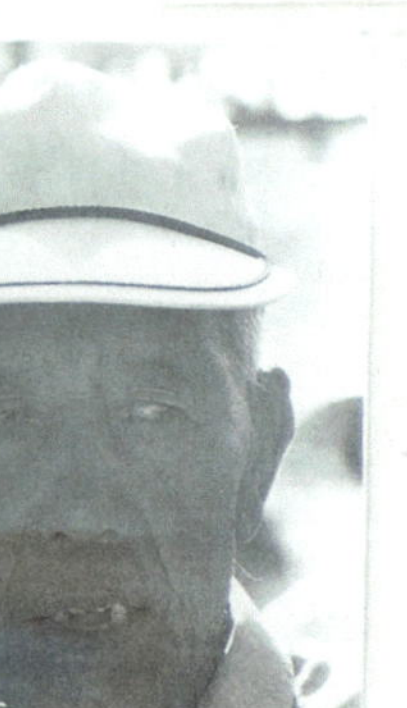

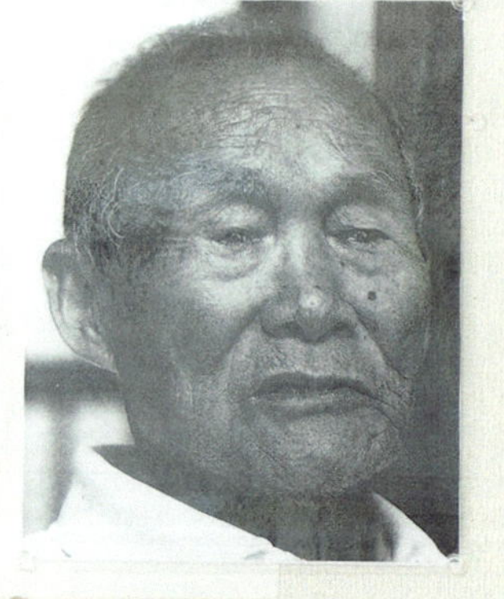

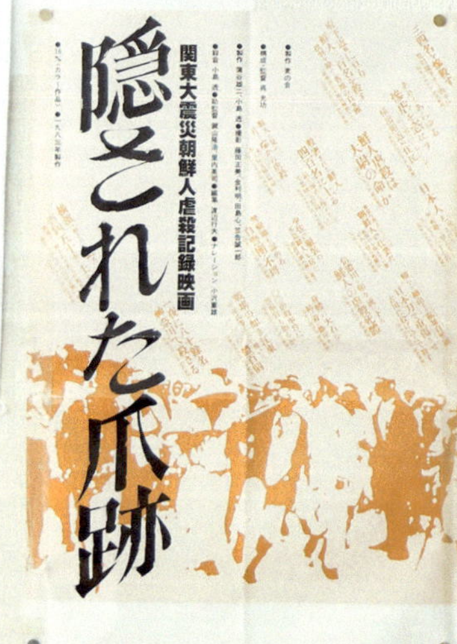

関東大震災朝鮮人虐殺記録映画
隠された爪跡
●一九八三年製作

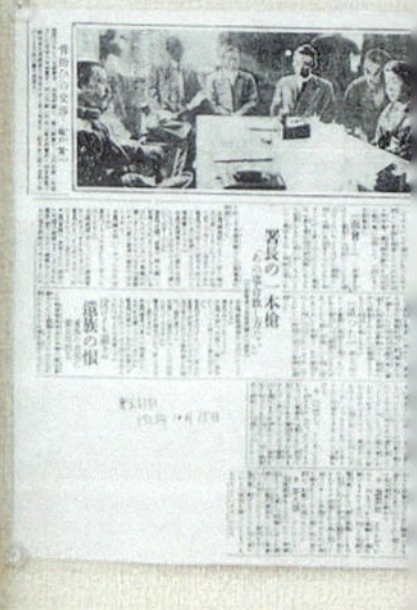

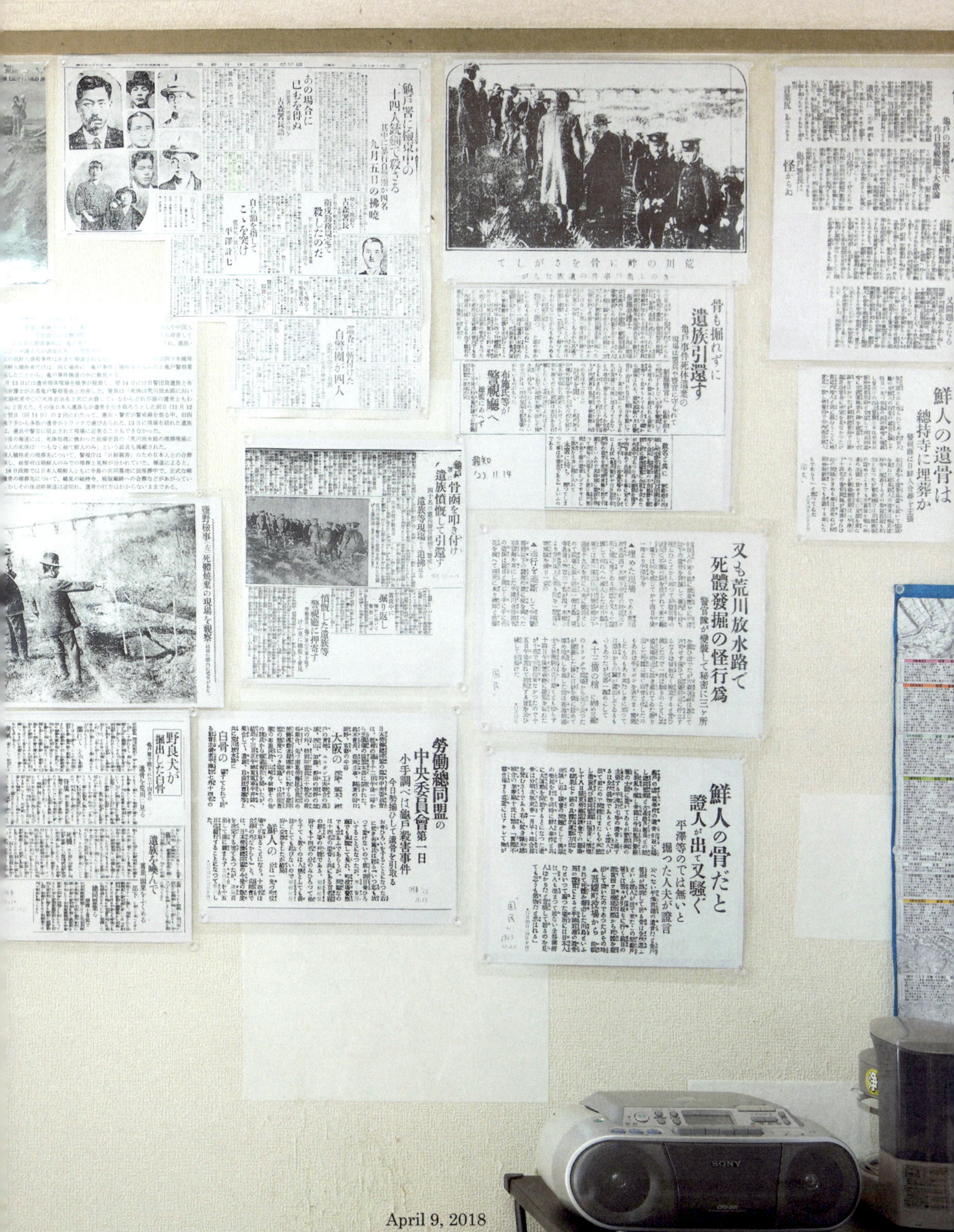

鮮人の遺骨は總持寺に埋葬か
又も荒川放水路で死體發掘の怪行爲
鮮人の骨だと證人が出て又騒ぐ
骨も掘れずに遺族引還す
勞働總同盟の中央委員會第一日
野良犬が掘出した白骨

April 9, 2018

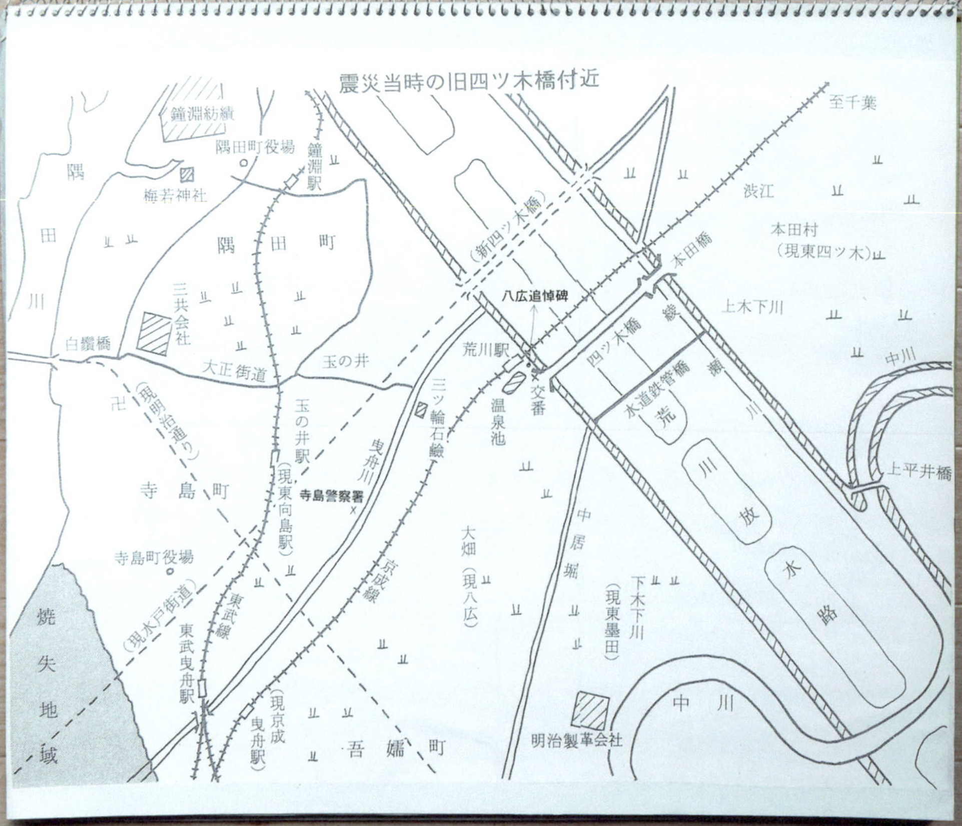

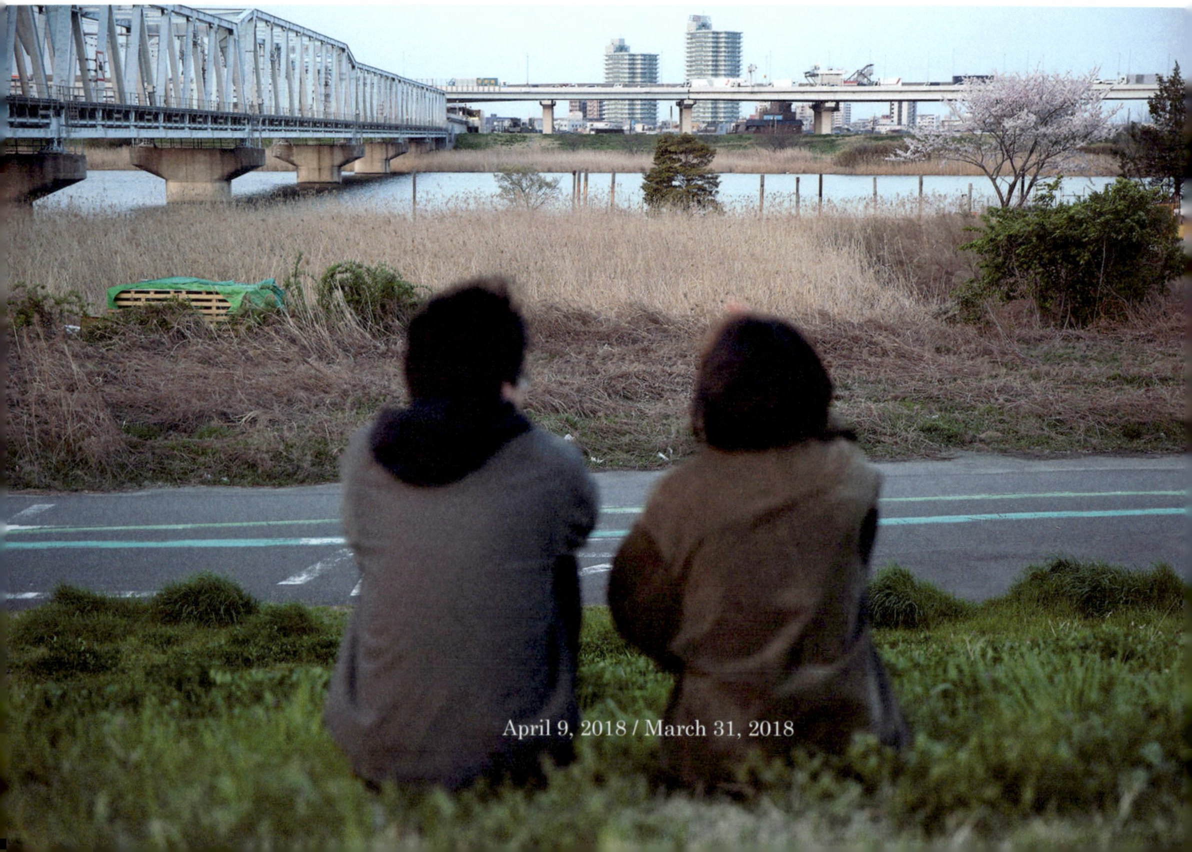

震災当時の旧四ツ木橋付近

鐘淵紡績
隅田町役場
鐘淵駅
至千葉
渋江
本田村（現東四ツ木）
隅田町
梅若神社
隅田川
隅　田　町
八広追悼碑
本田橋
上木下川
中川
三共会社
白鬚橋
大正街道
玉の井
（新四ツ木橋）
荒川駅
四ツ木橋
綾瀬川横断
水道鉄管橋
荒　川　放　水　路
（現明治通り）
卍
玉の井駅（現東向島駅）
三ツ輪石鹸
交番
温泉池
上平井橋
寺島町
寺島警察署
曳舟川
大畑（現八広）
中居堀
下木下川（現東墨田）
焼失地域
（現水戸街道）
寺島町役場
東武線
東武曳舟駅
京成線
（現京成曳舟駅）
吾嬬町
明治製革会社
中川

April 9, 2018 / March 31, 2018

On the Dead

When we think about "community," we probably have in mind the people who are actually living here and now. For example, the word *multicultural- ism* evokes images of a society where people from different backgrounds live together by mutually understanding their differences.

But suppose we were to think about a community with the dead? For example, we might carry with us the memory of someone who has died. Then something happens and we suddenly recall that person. What I think on such occasions is that this could be one way of living with the dead. It's the same with art history. Art history is the legacy of the fail- ures and achievements of artists who are no longer with us, and making art is one way to respond to the works left by the dead.

Standing at the site where the lynchings took place a hundred years before, and with many of the victims' remains still yet to be recovered, perhaps all we can do is use our imagination. It is hard to imagine the aftermath of the earthquake in the middle of what is now an idyllic land- scape (children play baseball, families go for walks, runners run by). Who could believe that so many Koreans—and also Chinese and Japanese— were killed here by mobs incited by demagoguery?

As the sun sets on the banks of the Arakawa, I ask Woohi and Christian to talk about death and the dead. Christian recalls the dead through asso- ciations with certain objects or places. Woohi speaks about her uncle, who left behind a room full of books. Her uncle's family has sold off most of the books, but now Woohi wants to know more about what he was reading.

The notion that memories of the dead reside in their possessions is similar to the tradition of *katamiwake,* or the distribution of memen- toes of the deceased. The idea is that, by sharing the things left by the deceased, the surviving family members and friends can recall the per- son through those objects.

April 3, 2018

SUNDAY, APRIL 1

 # Reference 1: Zainichi Koreans and Racism in Japan
I asked Tong-hyon Han to write a text for this catalogue providing background information on the *Zainichi* Koreans (see pp. 101–108 of this volume). For the film shoot, I had her present a mock lecture on the subject to an audience of extras.

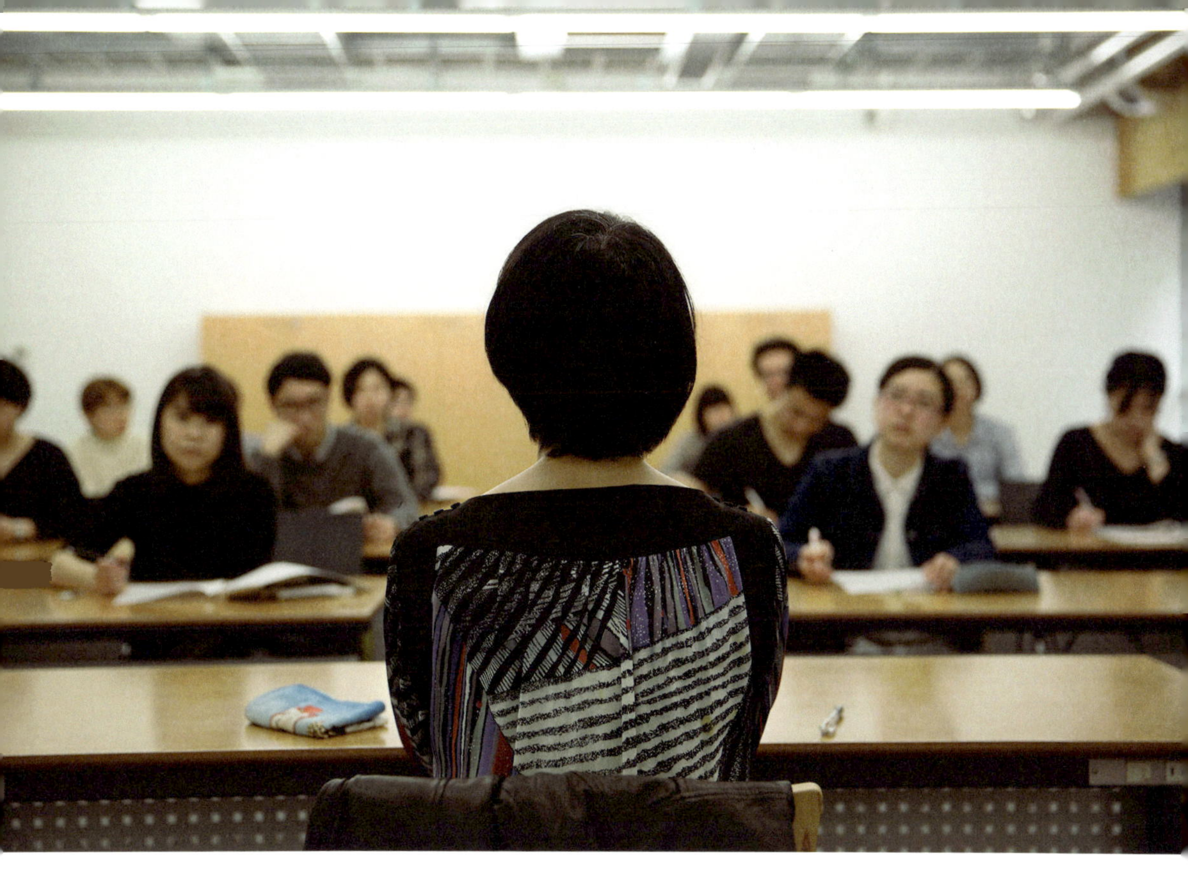

April 1, 2018

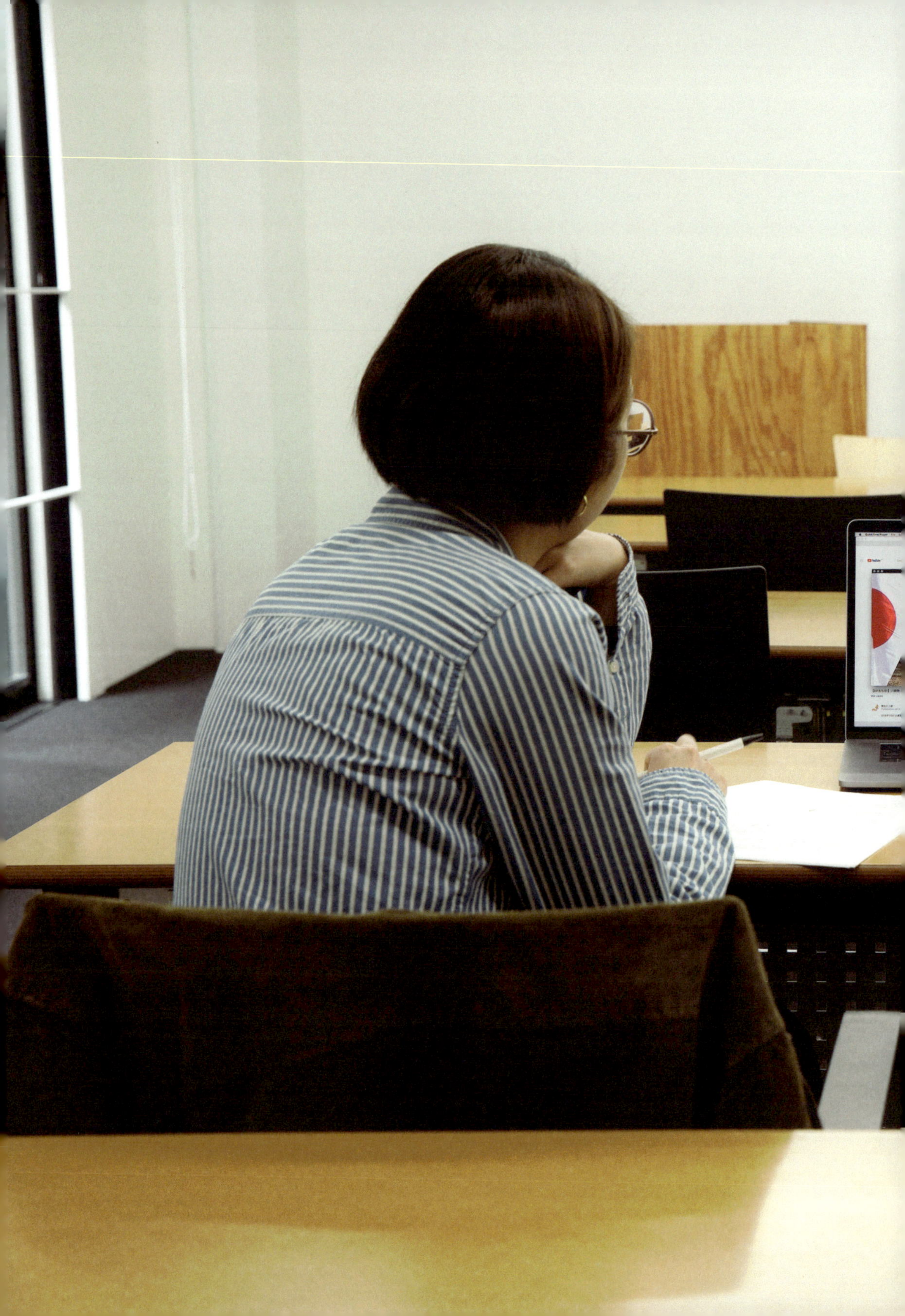

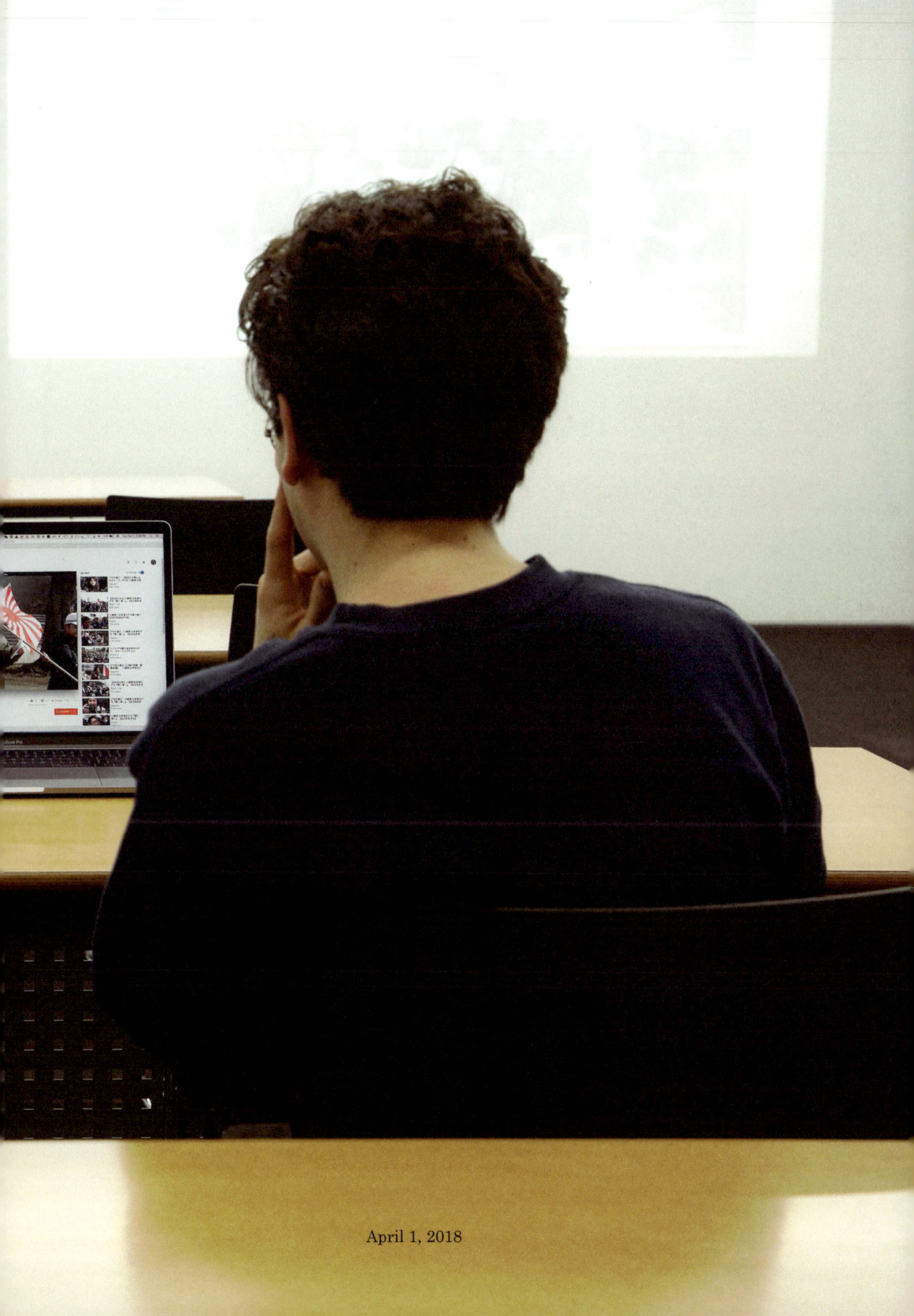

April 1, 2018

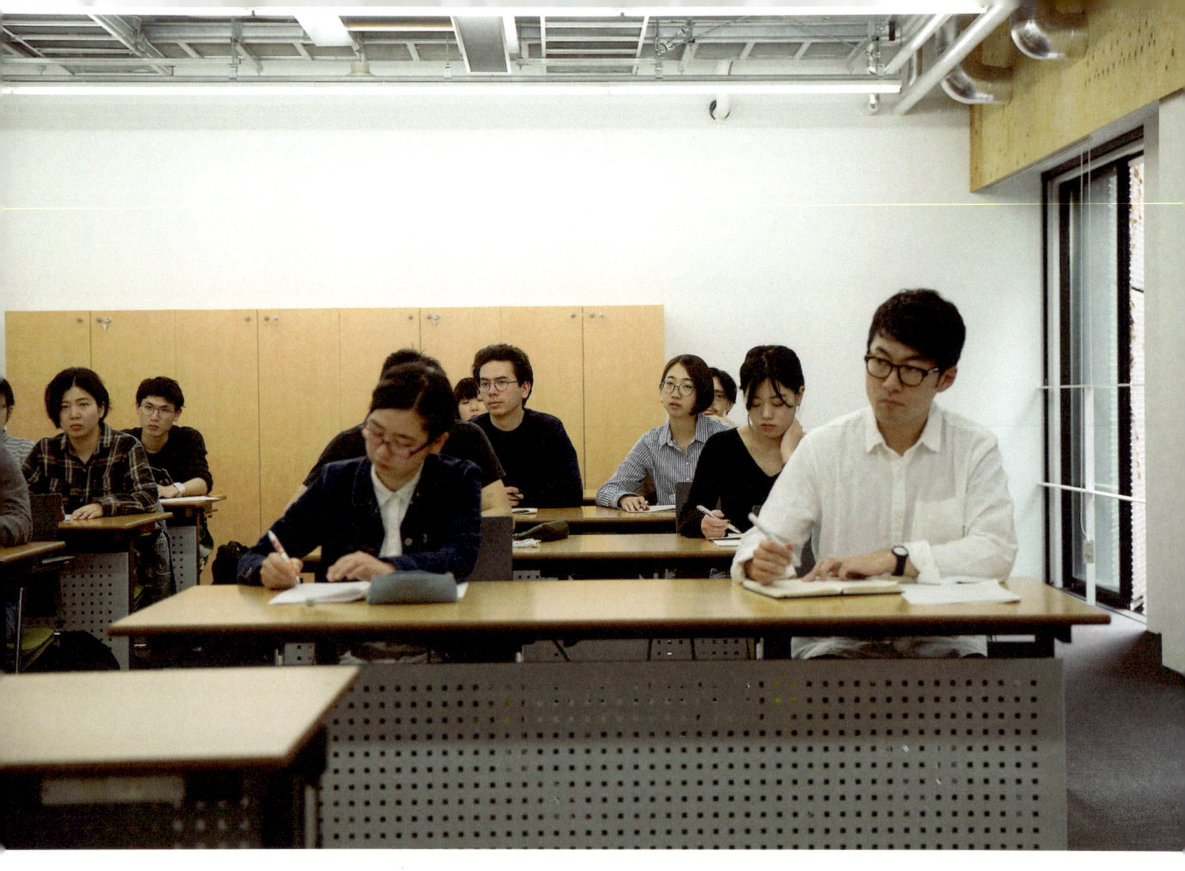

April 1, 2018

Reference 2: YouTube / Hate Speech

In advance of our visit to the site in Kawasaki where hate speech rallies took place, I had Woohi and Christian watch footage of the rallies on YouTube. Woohi said that when she listened to the stories about the lynchings of Koreans at Arakawa, she was able to stay cool because she could put some distance between herself and the past. But this time, upon hearing what was said at the rallies, she said she did not want to see or hear anymore. Brandishing not only the current national flag but also the imperial war flag and placards and banners, the people at the rallies spewed all kinds of vile language. During filming, we lowered the volume of the videos, or muted it entirely.

April 3, 2018

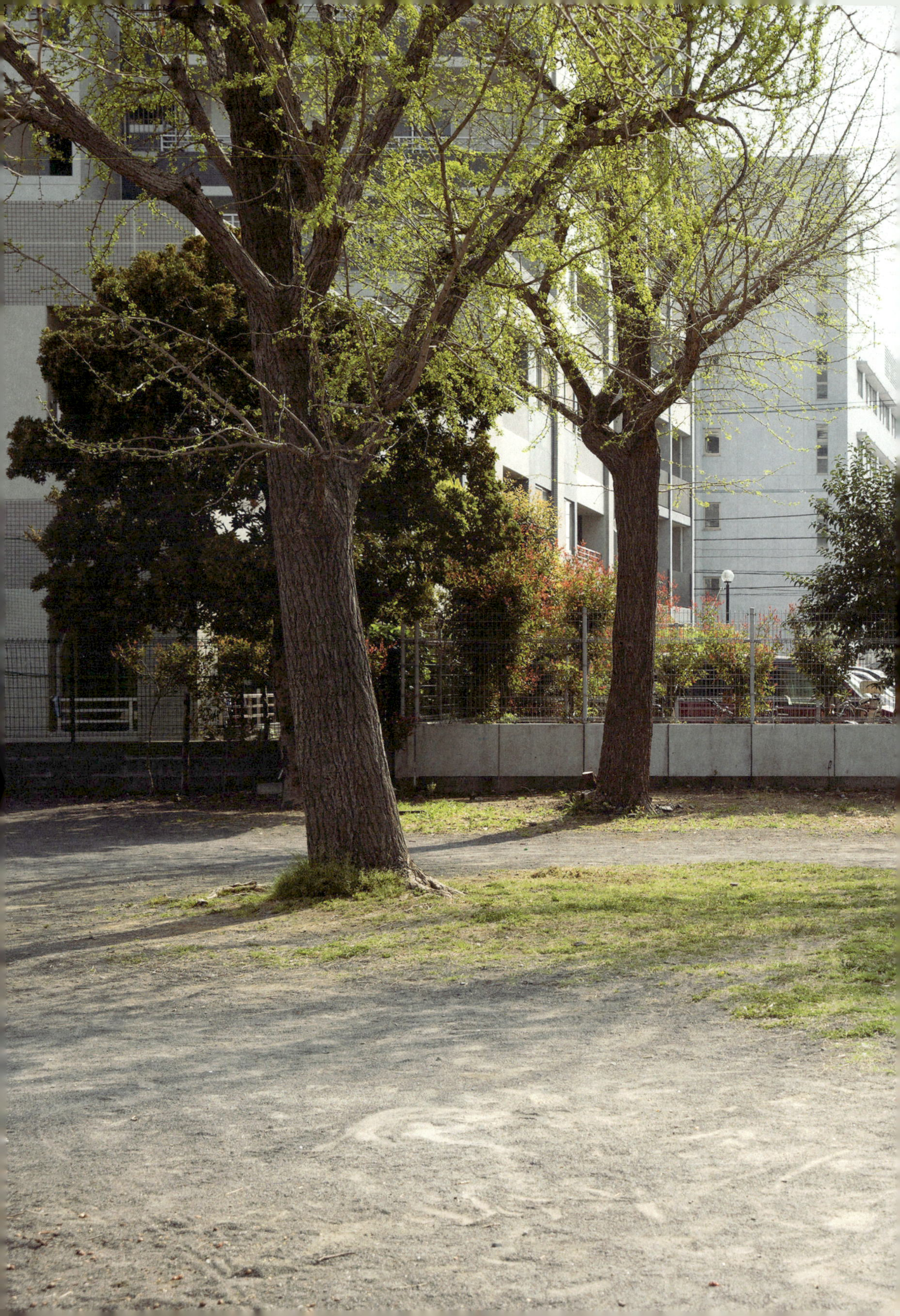

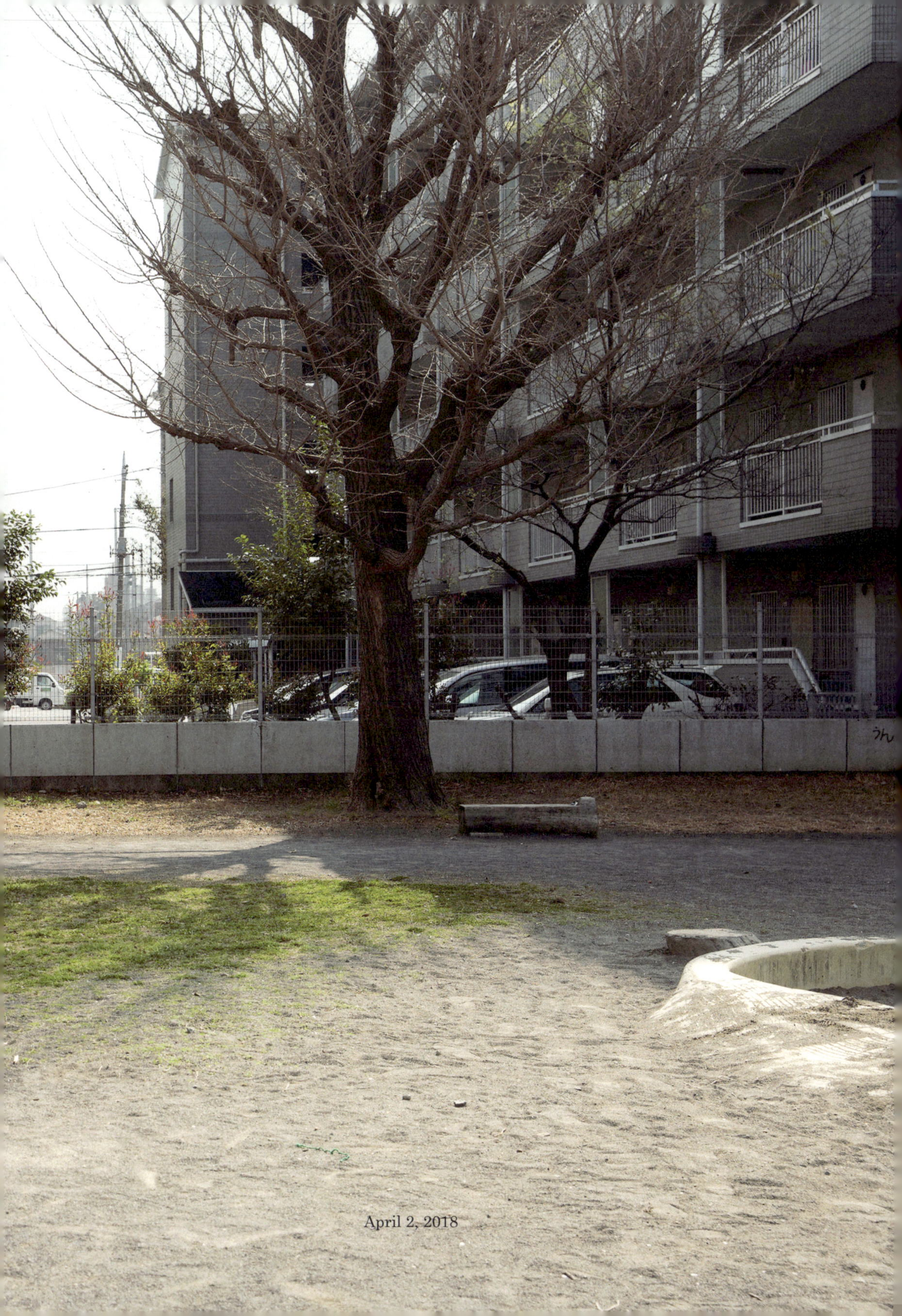

April 2, 2018

MONDAY, APRIL 2

 # In the Present—Visiting a Site 2: Reading the Law in Kawasaki
The residential neighborhood of Sakuramoto, in Kawasaki on the outskirts of Tokyo, is home to a *Zainichi* Korean community. To date, a number of hate speech rallies targeting *Zainichi* Koreans have been held at a local park there, Fujimi Park. The participants in the rallies say things like "Korea and North Korea are our enemies! Of course we're gonna tell our enemies 'Die!' and 'We'll kill you!' Korean cockroaches, get out!" or "Sakuramoto is Japan. Who's got a problem with us demonstrating here? They can get upset all they want—until they go crazy! 'Cause we're gonna tie up their necks and slowly strangle them—every one, until they're all gone from Japan!" or they hold up placards with the injunction "Kill!" written on them. Although the so-called "anti-hate speech law" that was passed in 2016 (The Act on the Promotion of Efforts to Eliminate Unfair Discriminatory Speech and Behavior against Persons Originating from Outside Japan) is a statement of principle only, with no penal provisions, it played a role in the decision of the Yokohama District Court's Kawasaki branch to issue a provisional injunction prohibiting the holding of hate speech rallies in Sakuramoto.

I had Woohi and Christian give readings of related laws and decisions at Fujimi Park, where the hate speech rallies took place, and at another site in Sakuramoto where counterprotestors and citizens had gathered to block the hate speech marchers from entering the neighborhood. The sociologist Takahiro Akedo selected the material for the readings: The Universal Declaration of Human Rights and the International Convention on the Elimination of All Forms of Racial Discrimination as basic materials concerning human rights; the Resolution on the Elimination of Hate Speech, which was issued by the House of Councilors' Committee on Judicial Affairs in order to clarify the scope of the "anti-hate speech law" after it was passed in the National Diet; the Rabat Plan of Action proposed by the Office of the United Nations High Commissioner for Human Rights (OHCHR); and the decision on the injunction prohibiting hate rallies. Woohi read in Japanese and Christian in English, but the legal language was difficult, and they had to do several takes each time.

April 3, 2018

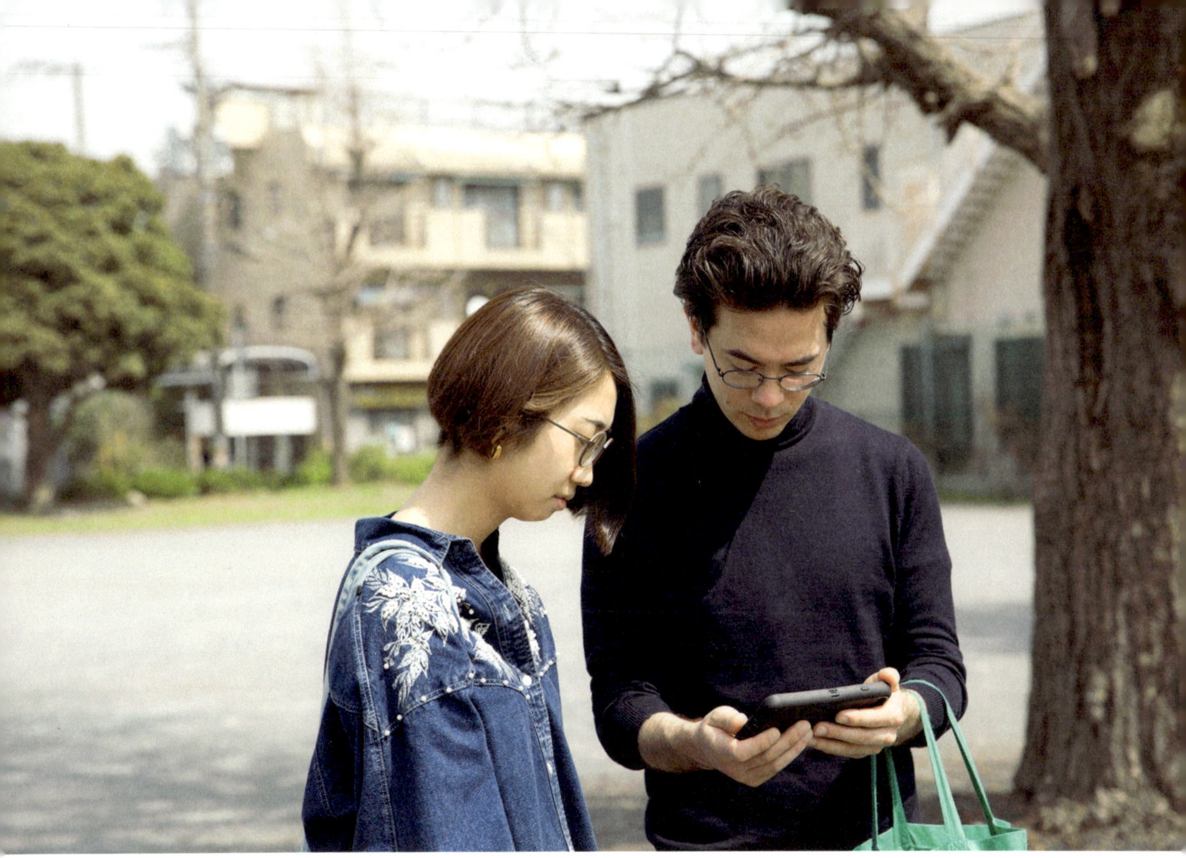

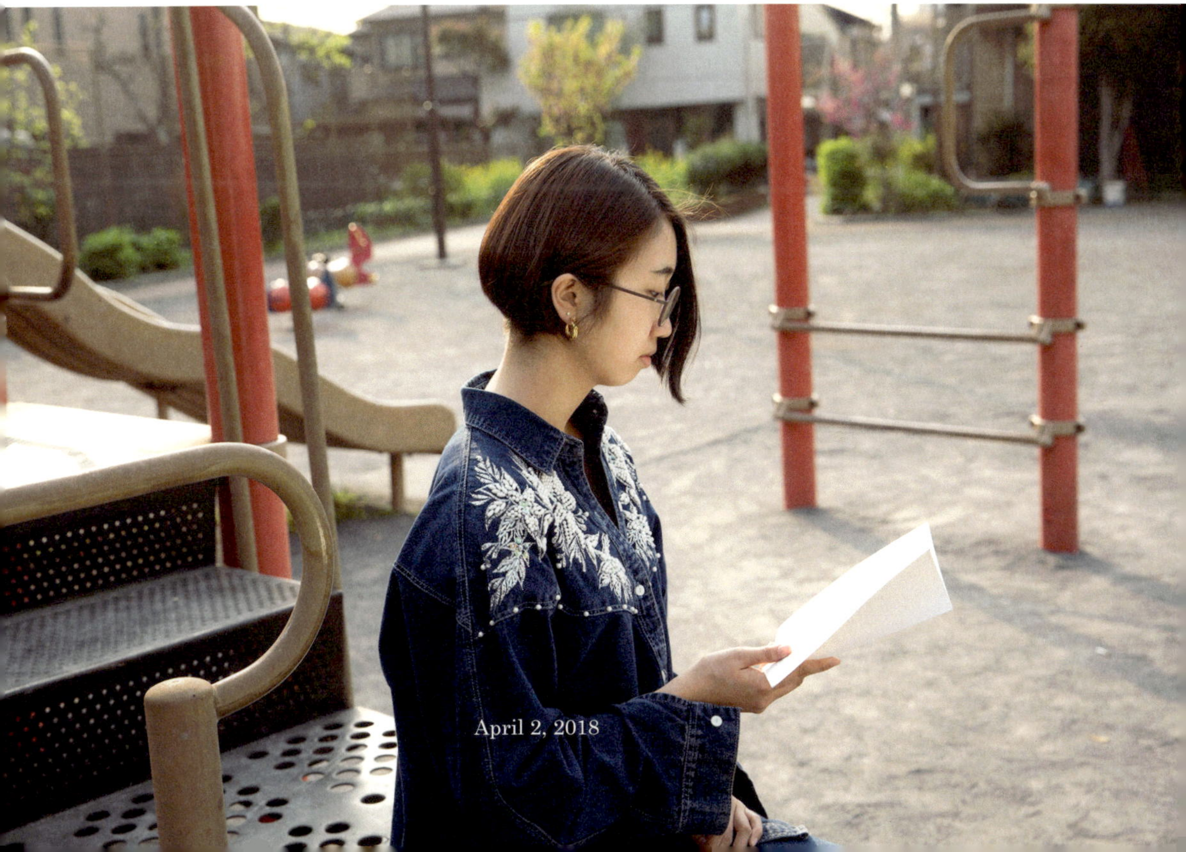

April 2, 2018

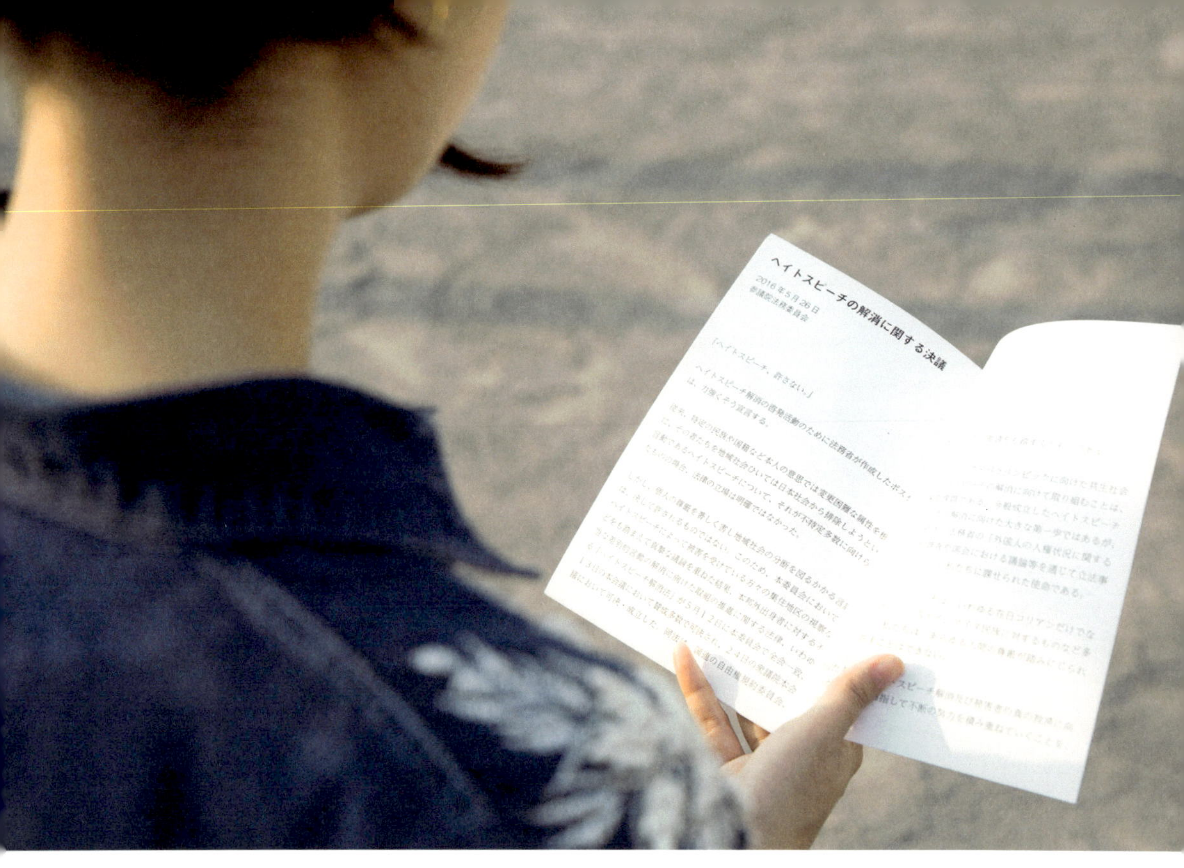

April 2, 2018

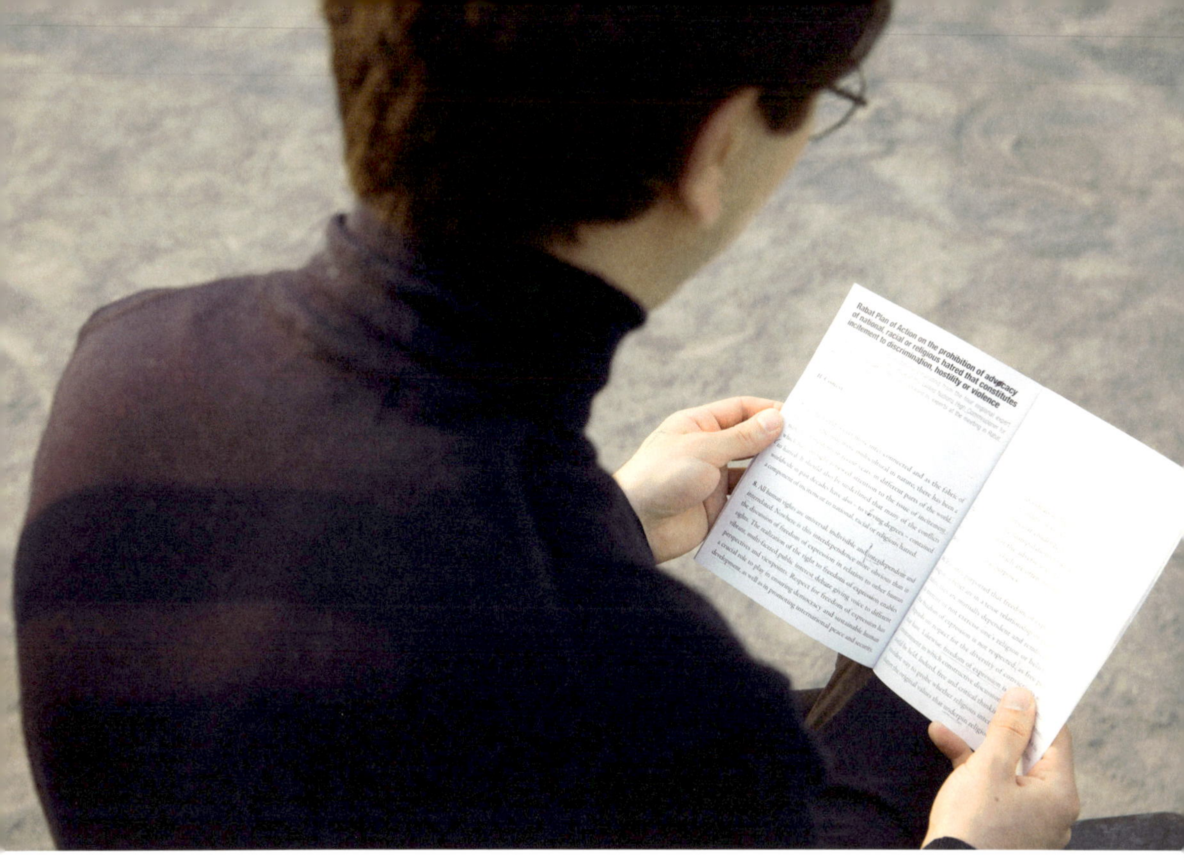
Rabat Plan of Action on the prohibition of advocacy
of national, racial or religious hatred that constitutes
incitement to discrimination, hostility or violence

April 2, 2018

Names

When do we feel we have been the object of discrimination?

Woohi has a Japanese name, Yuki. (In fact, her family and relatives generally call her by this name.) But when she uses her Korean name, she also reveals her origins. The racism of Japanese people tends to come up in trivial, everyday reactions. After they hear Woohi's Korean name, they might ask, "Do you like K-Pop?" or "Do you know any shops with good kimchee?" But beyond invoking such trivial cultural stereotypes, they might also respond with more malicious comments, such as "Hi, Kim Jong-un!"

Of course, if they were to go overseas, the Japanese people who invoke such cultural stereotypes might find themselves instead being stereotyped as Japanese or as Asians. Christian, who has Asian features, says that people sometimes see him and assume he is good at math.

These trivial, everyday reactions are not always malicious in intent. But invoking cultural stereotypes means that one is superficially judging and categorizing the other. Even when they are positive, such as when someone assumes Christian is good at math, these surface judgments are just one step removed from malicious and prejudicial discrimination.

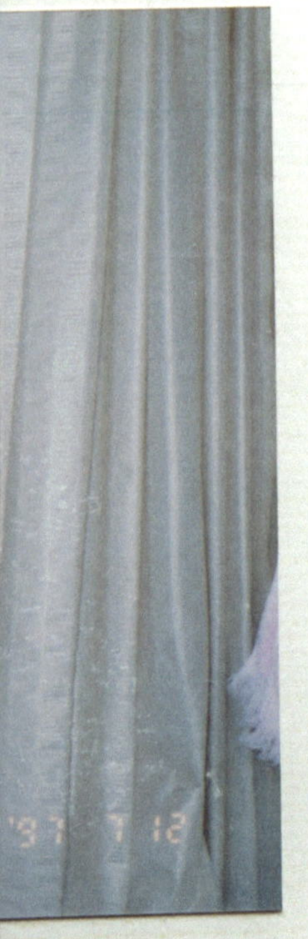
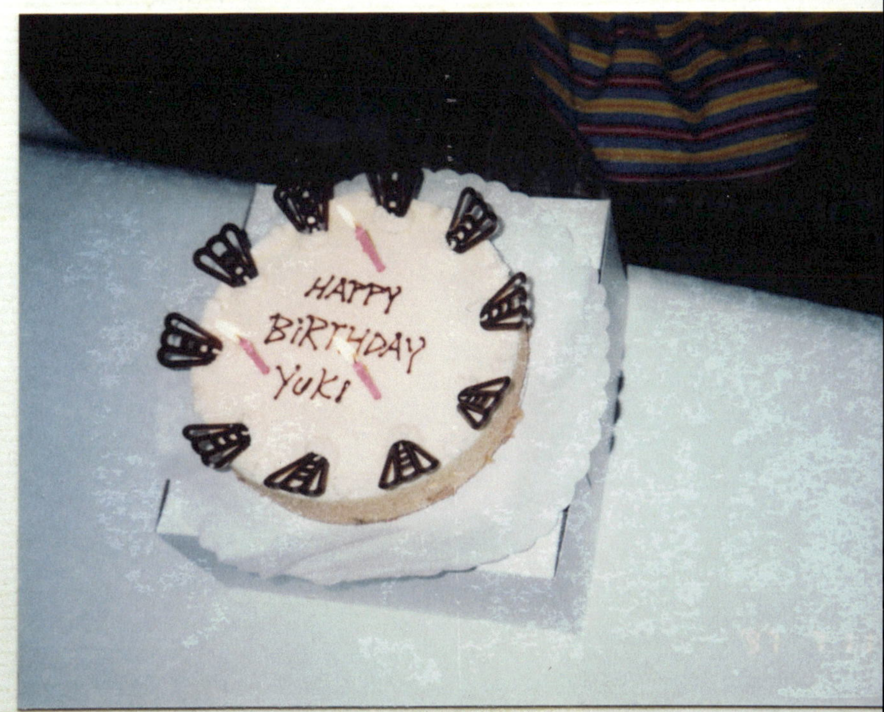

July 11, 1997

April 9, 2018

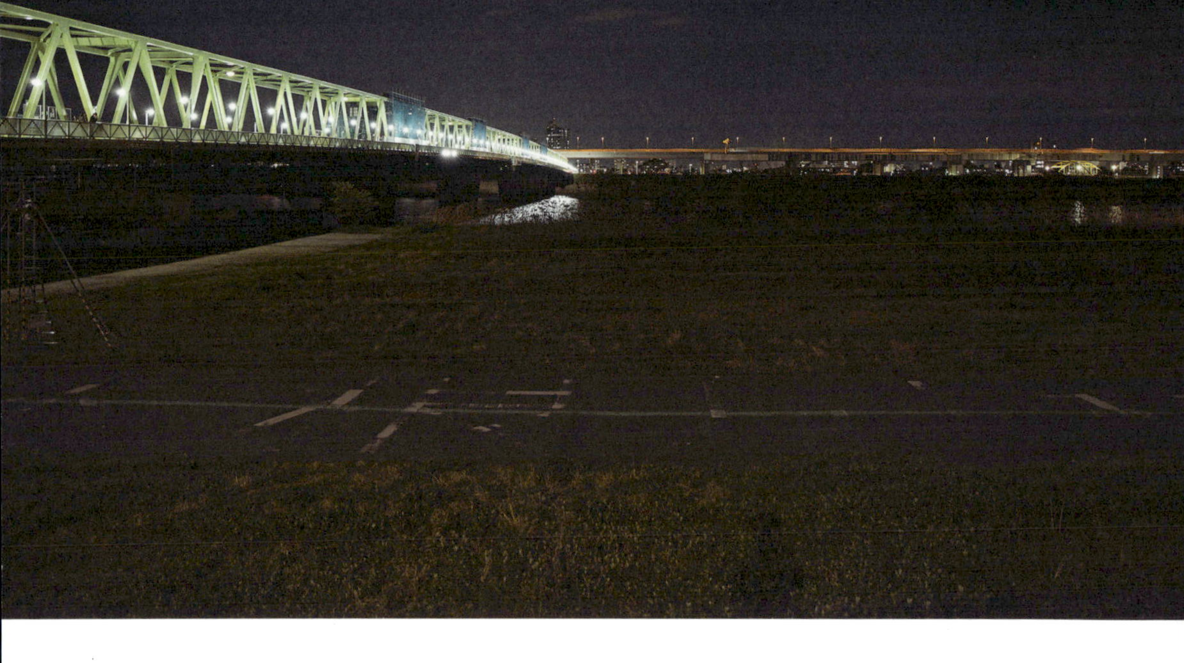

April 9, 2018

Silence

I came up with questions for Woohi and Christian as a way to introduce topics and ideas I wanted them to address: Do you have any uncomfortable moments in your life? Have you ever felt humiliated by someone? Has anyone ever called you something specific related to your background? When do you think you are your true self? How do you define yourself? What if a disaster happened here—do you think people would be willing to help each other?

The two tried to respond to the questions in their own words. But sometimes they seemed to get stuck, and then they would fall silent. Or maybe they were just tired after a long day of filming. The words stopped. But even when the silence continued, I decided to wait just a bit longer, without rushing things. Because sometimes the silence leads to renewed conversation.

FRIDAY, APRIL 6

 # Arrival: On Acting

I felt the scene where Christian arrives and Woohi meets him at the airport was necessary to show Christian coming to Japan as an "other." Originally, the plan was for the crew to go to the airport on the day of Christian's actual arrival and film him walking through the gate. But we couldn't get permission to film that day, so we ended up having to shoot the "arrival scene" at a different airport later on in the course of production.

When we film I have been asking Woohi and Christian to repeat certain things for the cameras. For example, in the arrival scene I had them reenact their first meeting. They had to recall what happened the first time they saw each other a week earlier, and act as if there were still some awkwardness between them.

But there were other scenes, too. Sometimes I had them repeat things they had said during a production meeting once more for the camera, or I would ask the same question several times. Through these acts of repetition, words that were spoken unconsciously became conscious statements, and in viewing their behavior objectively, or at least relatively, Woohi and Christian could define their positions. That is, acting oneself also has an aspect of forming oneself. So how have they been affected by the experience of acting themselves?

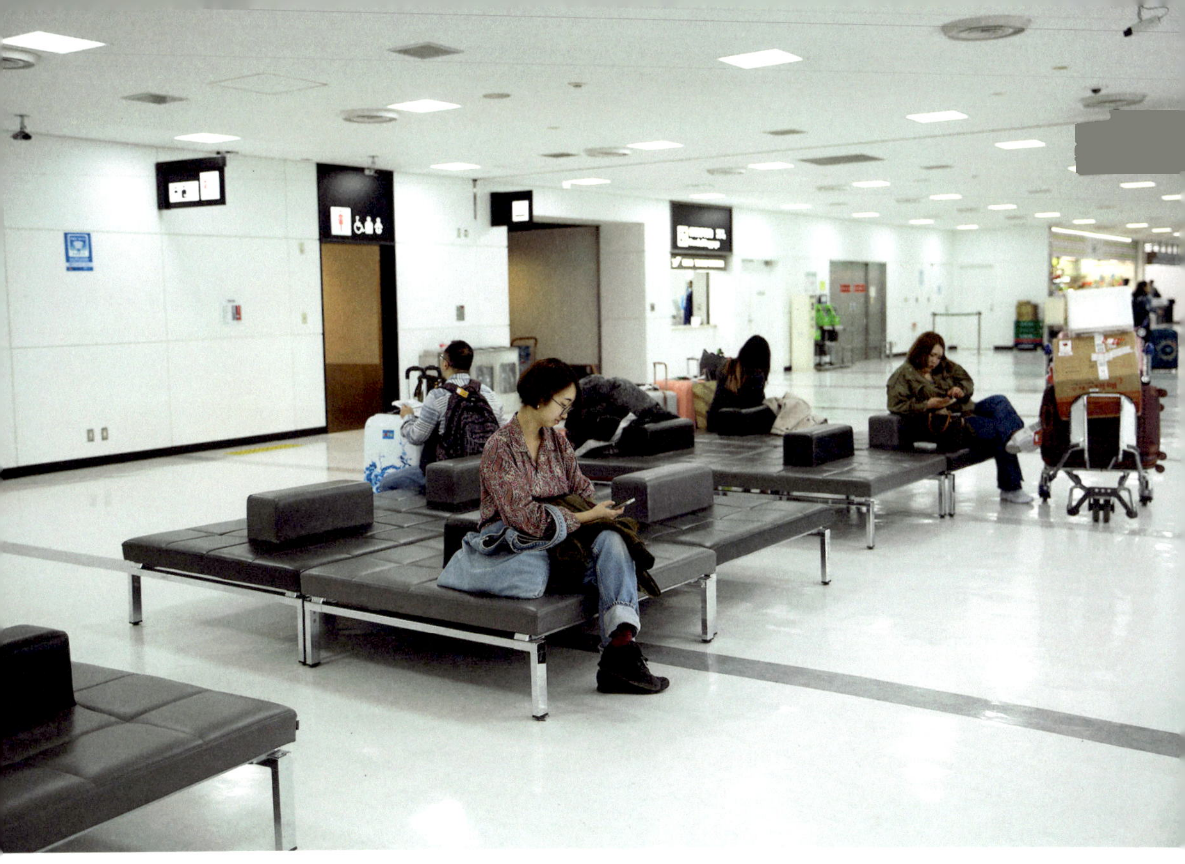

April 6, 2018

SATURDAY, APRIL 7

 # Interview as Exchange of Personal Histories: The Scent of Lemon
I enjoy driving and traveling in cars, but I can't stand riding in the back seat of a two-door car. Where are the doors for the back seat? It's impossible for me to sit still when I feel there is no way to open the door and get out on my own.

Woohi said she feels constricted in cars—so during filming we kept the windows open for most of the takes. But despite having the car windows open, the location we rented was not very spacious, the air inside did not circulate so well, and it quickly got stagnant. One of the crew members, Saki, had the idea of getting a lemon and squeezing its juices. We ended up placing lemon slices in the car and in the corners of the room. The citrus scent wafted faintly through the space, and it appeared that Woohi could relax a bit.

The inside of the car was a very intimate space. It was meant to function as a mechanism for Woohi and Christian to talk about things they had been unable to talk about: Woohi's ambivalence about identity, and Christian's nonchalance toward identity. With his Swiss father and Japanese American mother, Christian has a complex background. But for him that background is just one of his constitutive parts, and nothing to get anxious about. What he finds to be of more importance are his personal interests and the state of the surrounding culture. In that sense nationalism probably has no meaning to him.

Prompted by Christian, Woohi began to talk about the complexities of the *Zainichi* Korean community. Woohi attended both a pro–North Korea *Chōsen* school (the same as her mother had attended) and a South Korea–affiliated school for Korean nationals. But her father went to an ordinary Japanese school and uses his Japanese name. These different educational experiences complicate the *Zainichi* Korean identity. Whether to go by one's Korean or Japanese name; whether to speak the official Korean of South Korea, or the Korean taught at the *Chōsen* schools; whether to join one *Zainichi* Korean community or another, or to distance oneself from them altogether: Woohi is torn between the different communities that shaped her.

April 11, 2018

What impressed me the most was when Woohi said that, amid all these multiple communities, she does not want to "deny" her family or the friends she made at the different schools she attended. Typically, a community has clear boundaries and is reinforced by dynamics of exclusion and inclusion; there are times when one's community may be antagonistic toward another. Woohi said that she wished that her cousin who lives in the United States could understand the complexity of her position. This gives speaking in English extra significance for her. Maybe at the same time that she was explaining her situation to Christian in English, she was also addressing her cousin.

April 11, 2018

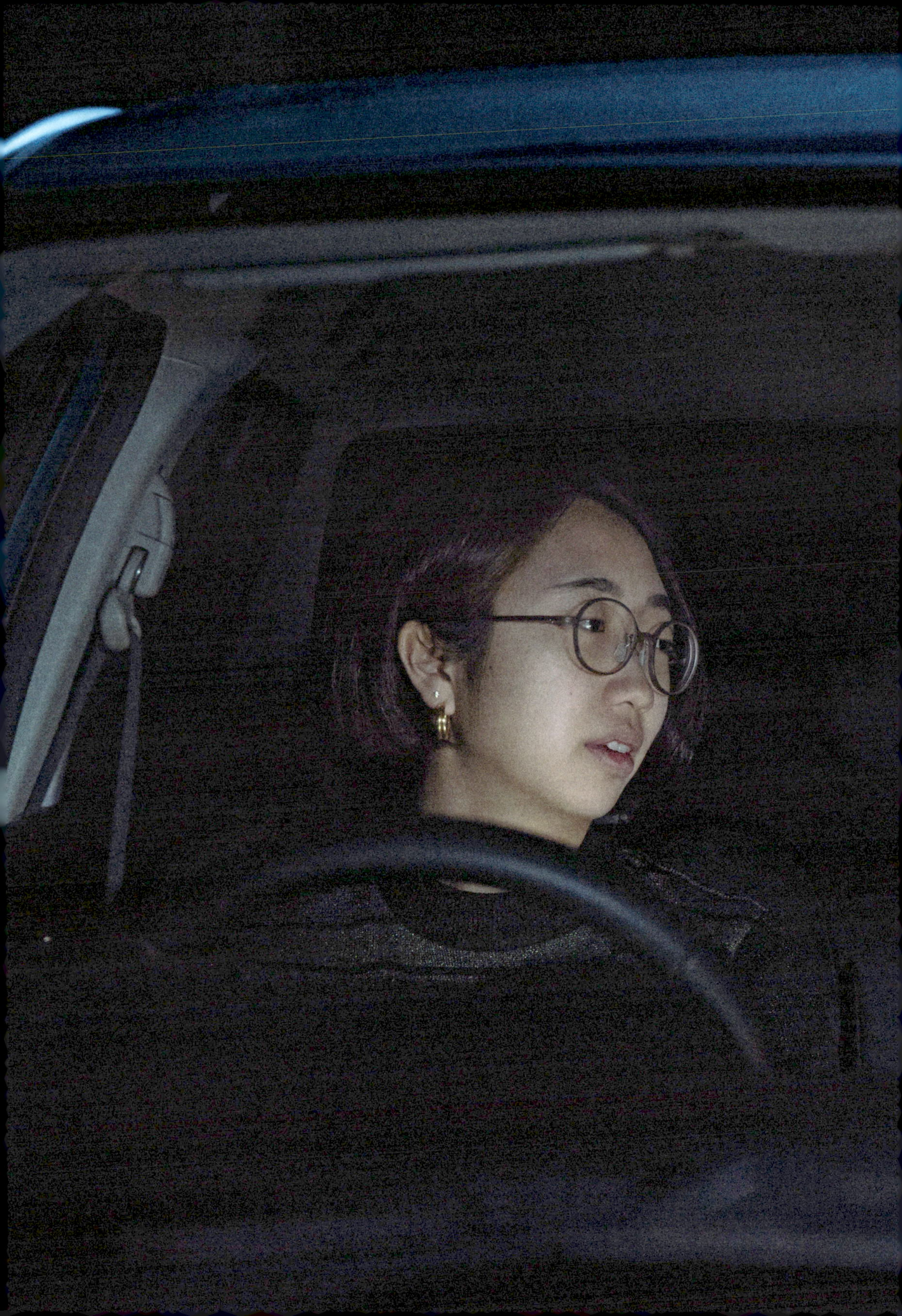

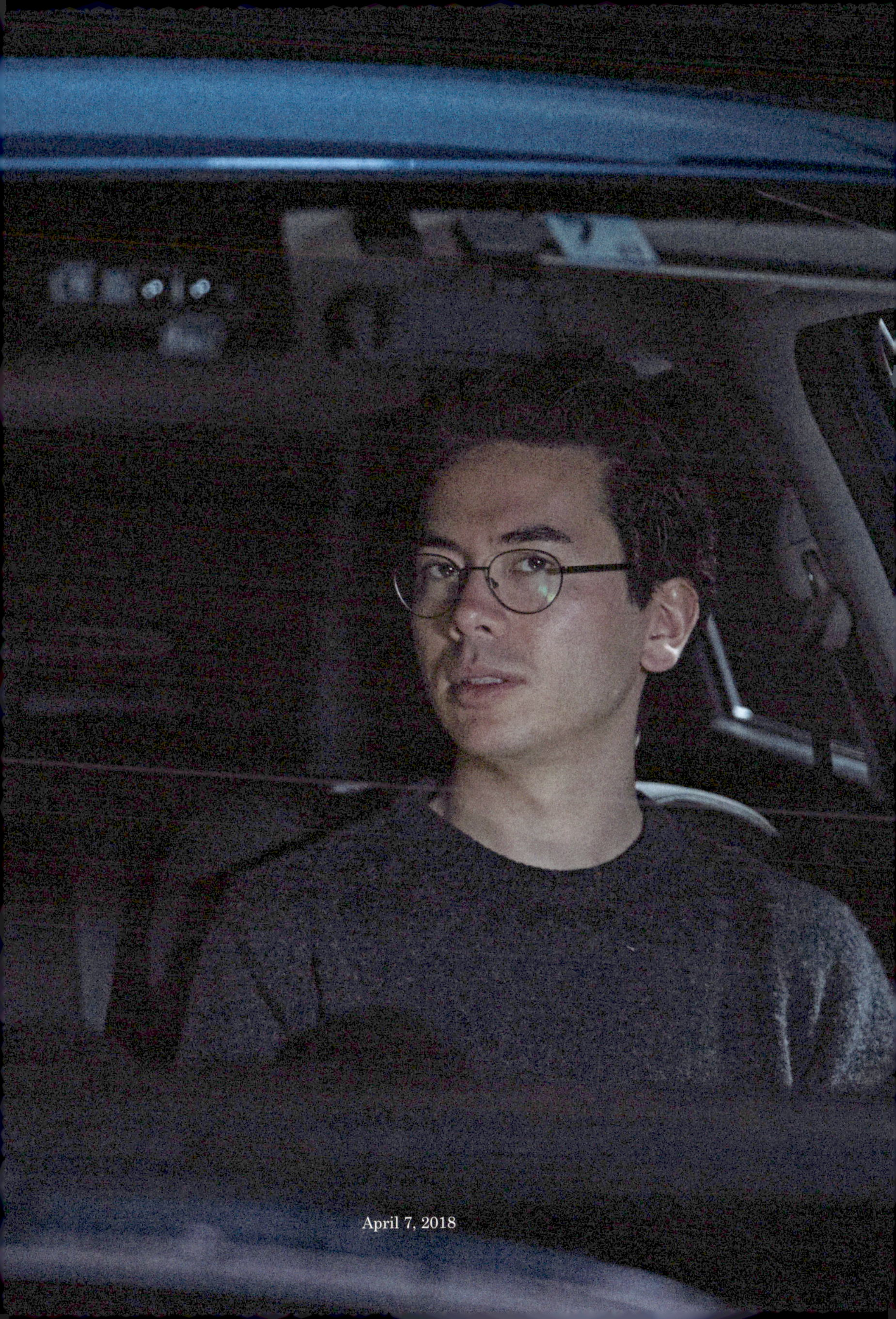
April 7, 2018

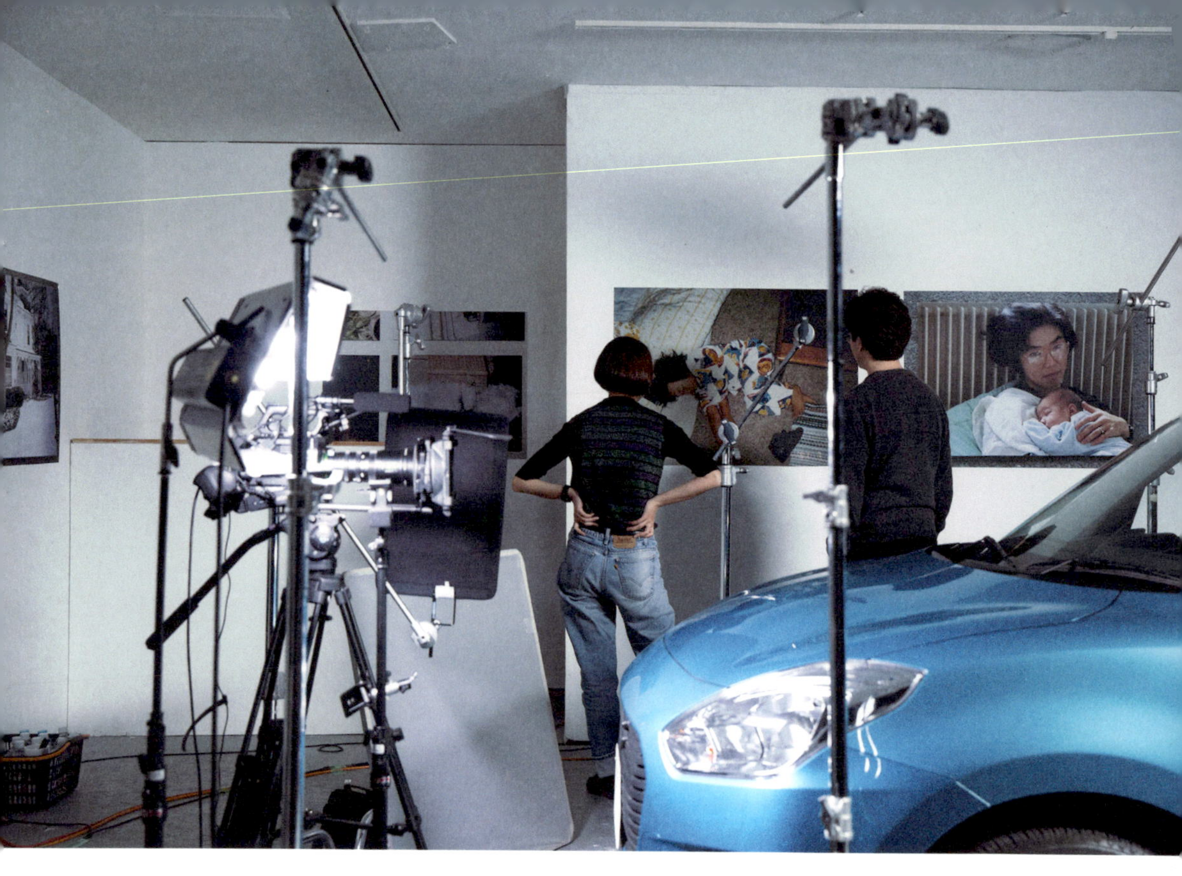

April 7, 2018

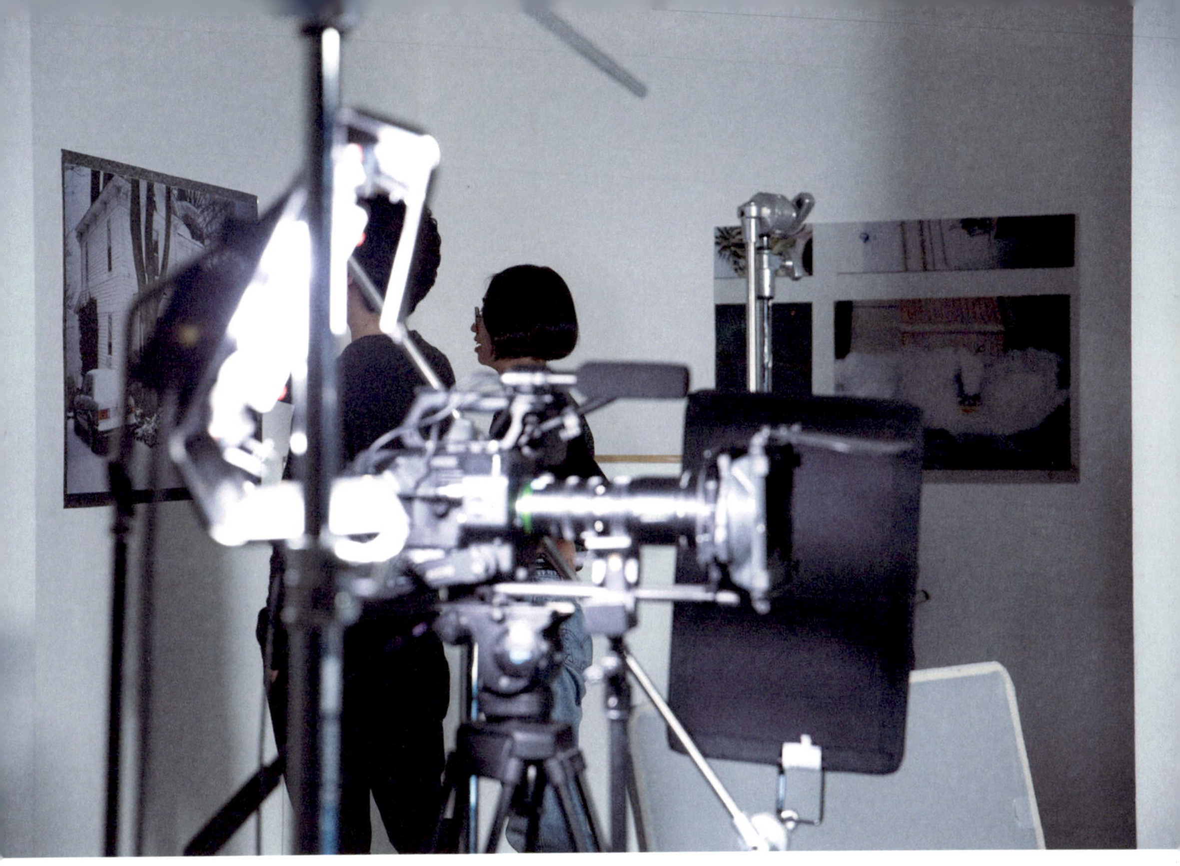

April 7, 2018

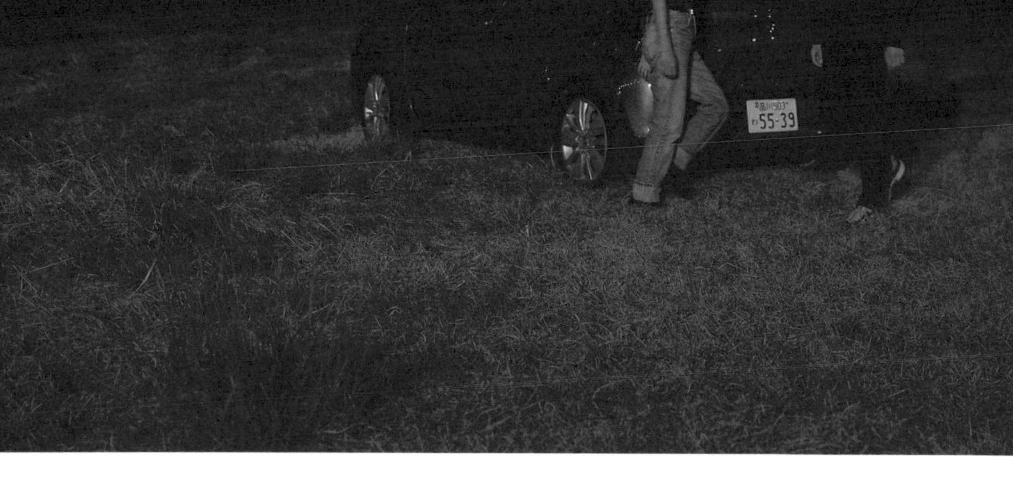

April 9, 2018

SUNDAY, APRIL 8

The Emancipated Camera

Tong-hyon Han suggested having a day for Woohi and Christian to decide their own activities. Certainly, the two would be spending the entire time over the course of production before the camera, thinking about and discussing the topics and questions I would pose to them. So I thought it made sense to provide them a day to act freely—outside the frame. They could escape the control of the director and move around as they like. And I could give them a handycam to film what they like.

After discussing several options, the pair chose the following places to visit: the Meiji Memorial Picture Gallery, with its paintings depicting key moments in the life of the Meiji Emperor, including the 1910 annexation of Korea by Japan; the observatory at Tokyo Tower, which offers a panorama over central Tokyo; and the Jinbocho district, where there are many used bookstores and antiquarians. In the end they ran out of time and couldn't make it to the bookstore district.

Reflective Bar

I wanted the last scene to be a moment for self-reflection. I chose a bar for the setting in order to visualize my position in the project through an architectural/spatial mise-en-scène. When we filmed the other scenes, I always stood next to the camera as an observer, watching the protagonists as they spoke and throwing topics at them from there. At the bar, I was on the inside of the counter while Woohi and Christian sat on the opposite side. Then once the three of us finished talking, I took over Christian's seat, Tong-hyon Han took over Woohi's seat, and Tong-hyon Han and I spoke together.

Tong-hyon Han was my interlocutor throughout the process of developing this project, listening to my ideas and giving me advice in the preparatory stages. She had participated in one of my previous projects. Had I never met her, this project might not have happened.

One thing she asked me about at the bar was how I could generalize the locally specific and private topic of *Zainichi* Koreans into something that could be understood by audiences who are far removed from the issue. I think the key to achieving this lies in the acting (of oneself) and the fictional aspects of the work—but I'm not sure how clearly I expressed it.

April 11, 2018

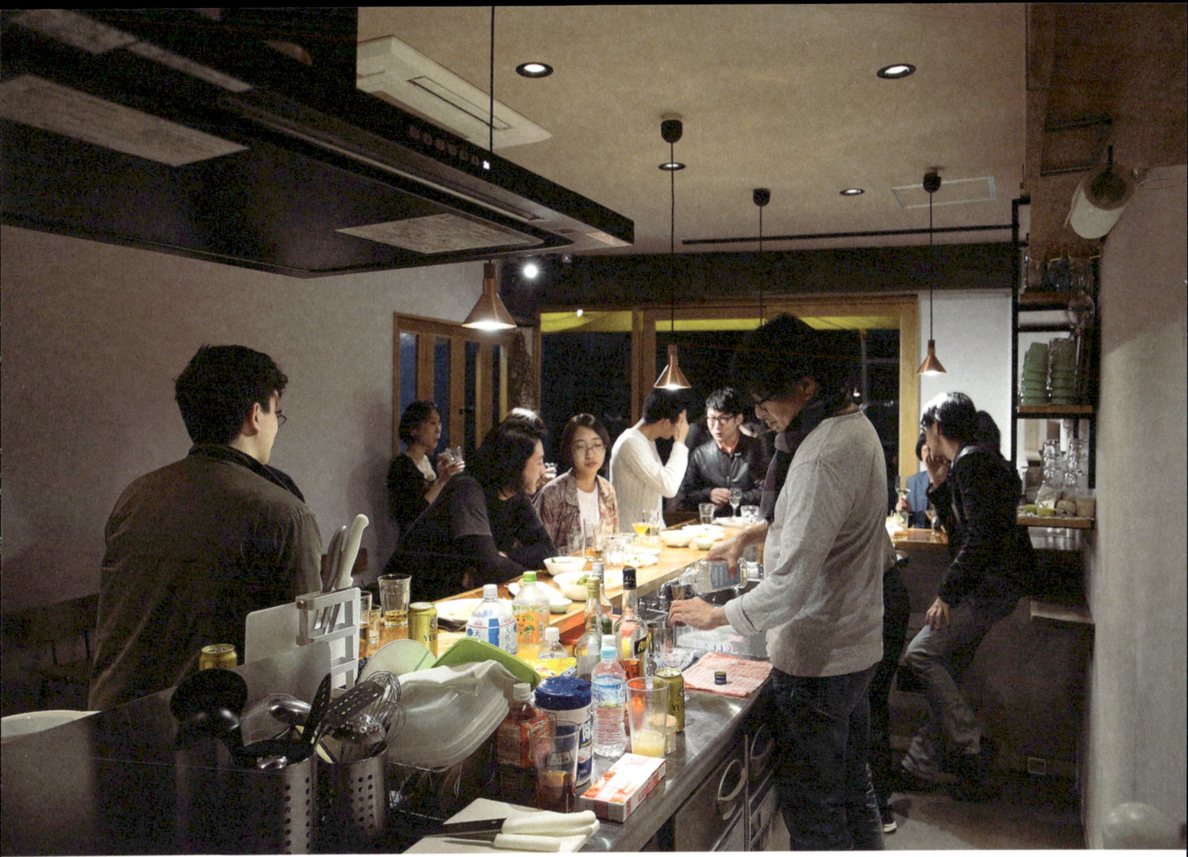

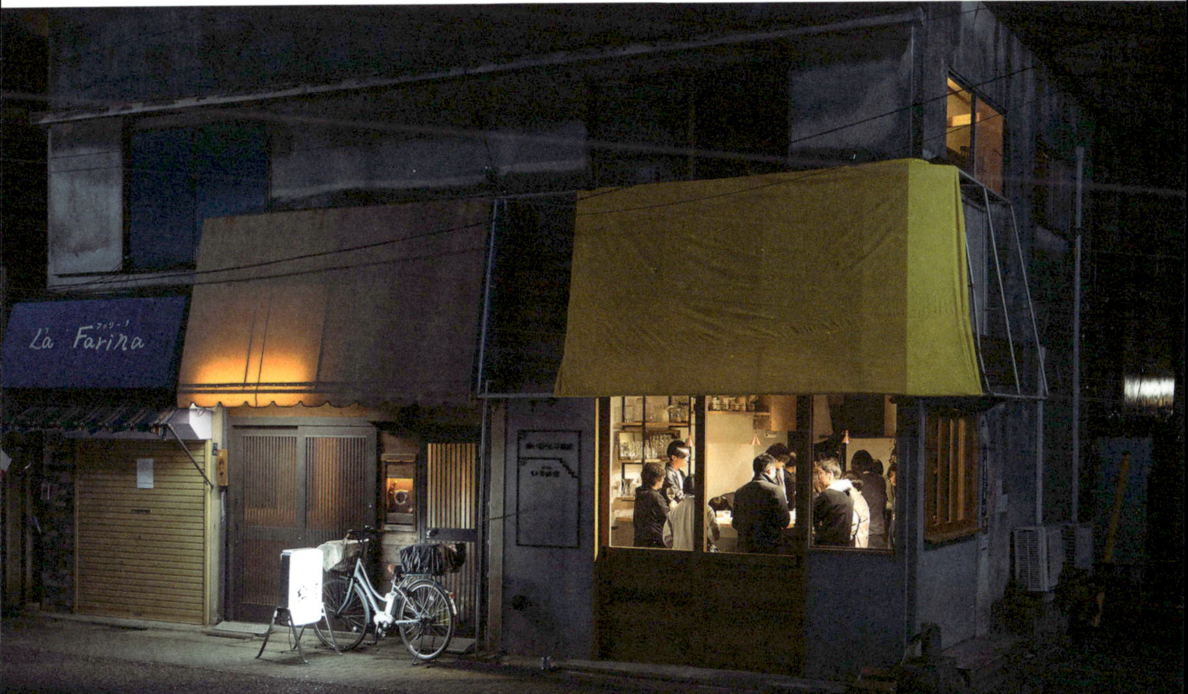

La Farina

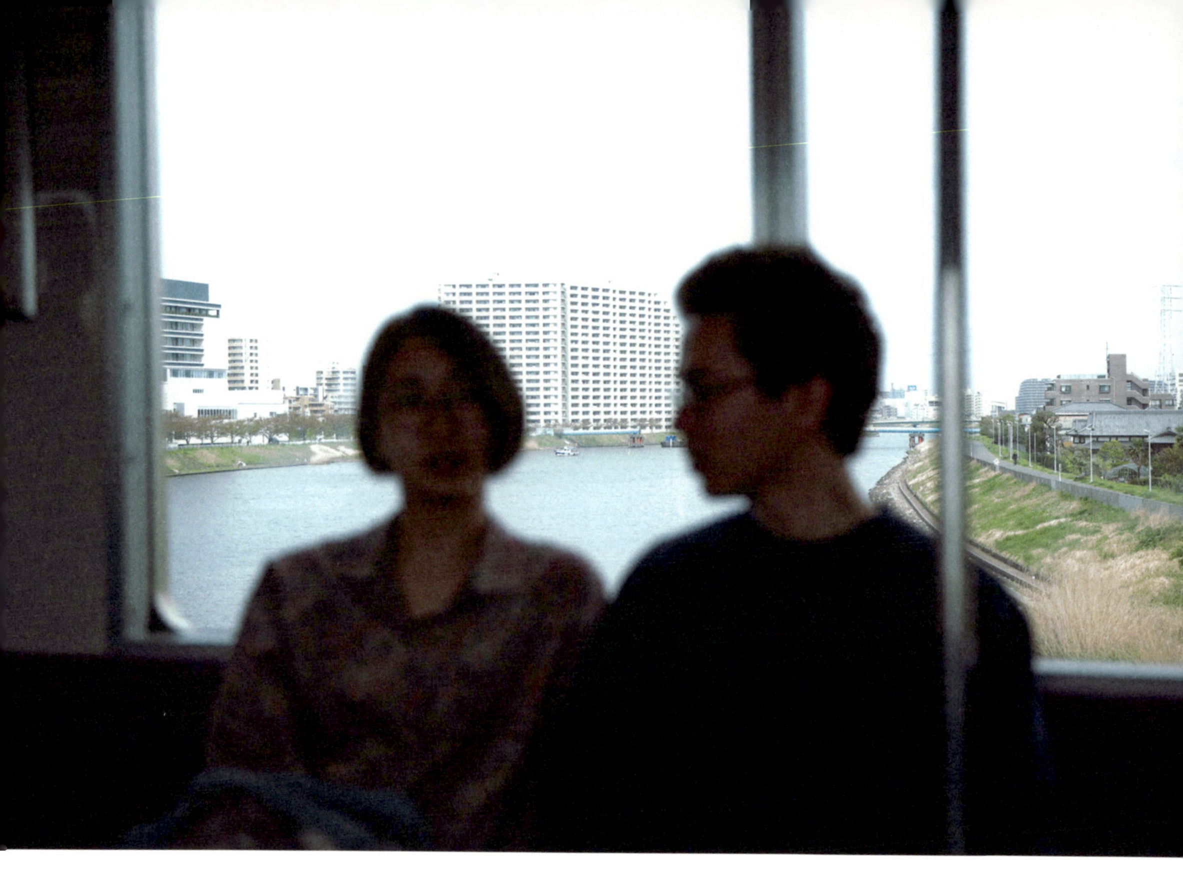

April 6, 2018

MONDAY, APRIL 9

 # Vulnerable Narrator

One of the most challenging issues of the post–March 2011 (or post-Fukushima) situation in Japan is the question of who is authorized to speak about the disaster. For example, when someone states "I am from Fukushima," it is a declaration of his or her proximity to the issue, and an assertion of the right to speak about "Fukushima" as an authority, as it were. But the more removed one is from the issue, the harder it is to speak about it.

I was not in Japan when the disaster struck. Nor am I from Fukushima or the vicinity of the disaster zone. As someone who was not affected directly, I find it difficult to talk about the disaster or the nuclear accident—because whatever I say could be easily criticized. When I address the topic of the disaster from my position of relative distance, people might think I am attempting to use it opportunistically. Even so, I've given a lot of thought to how to take responsibility for an issue that is "not my own" and yet still touches us all in some way.

Addressing the topic of the *Zainichi* Koreans involves a similar problem. In Japan, I am a member of the majority. Even if I am not *Zainichi* Korean, I am implicated in their experience as someone who belongs to the majority/those who might discriminate against the *Zainichi* Korean minority. The structure is more complex than that of Fukushima. There is a risk that it could lead to the appropriation of a minority issue by the majority. You might even criticize me for doing just that.

It's hard to engage with highly subjective issues as an outsider. On the other hand, being an outsider in a sense allows for some "room" toward the issue. And I feel a responsibility as someone with this "room." Because it is the one who has "room" who can step into a position where it is difficult to speak. To share the vulnerability of the subject. To imagine oneself in the place of the other. And yet to speak without fear. Do you think you can do that? I wonder whether I was able to do it this time.

April 11, 2018

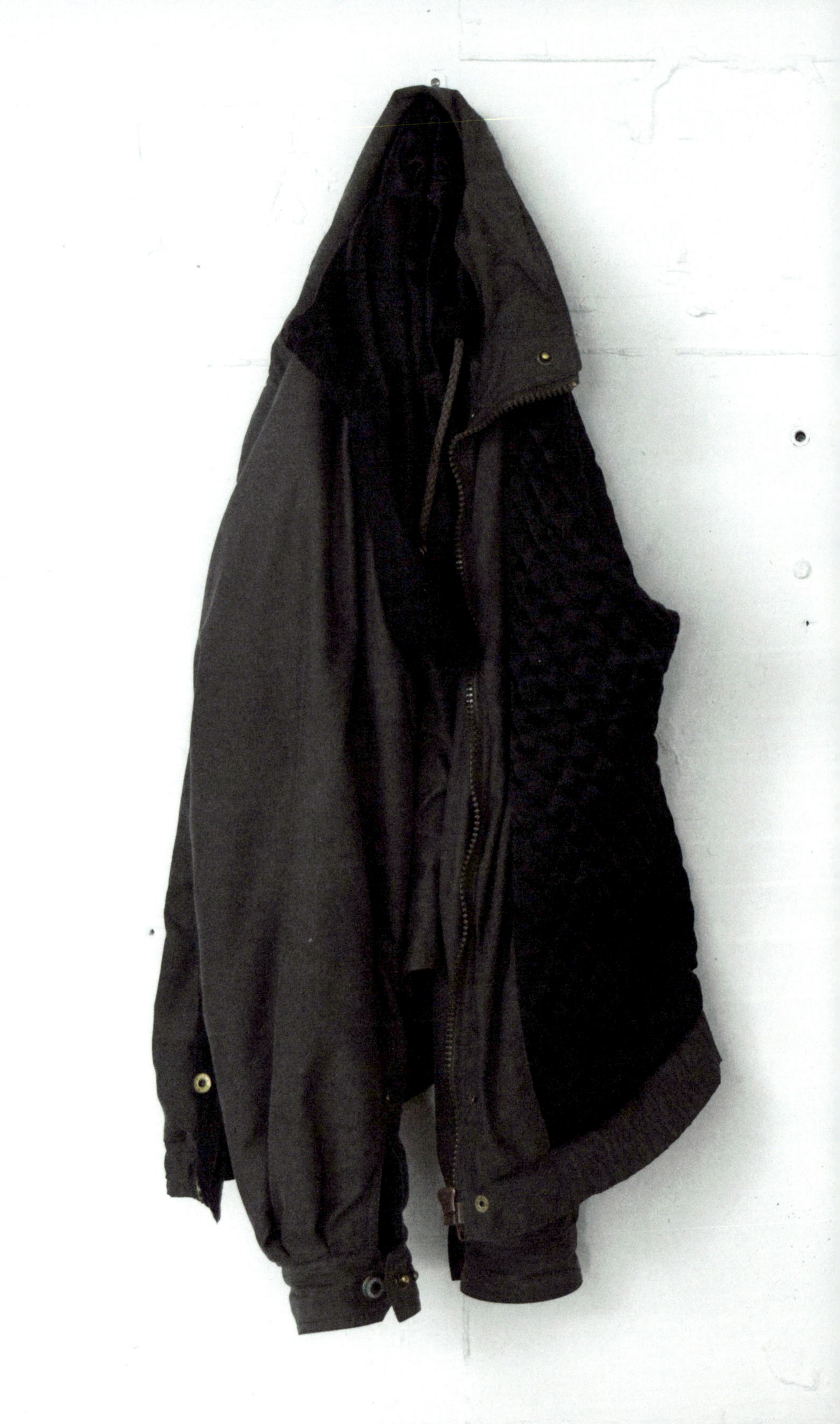

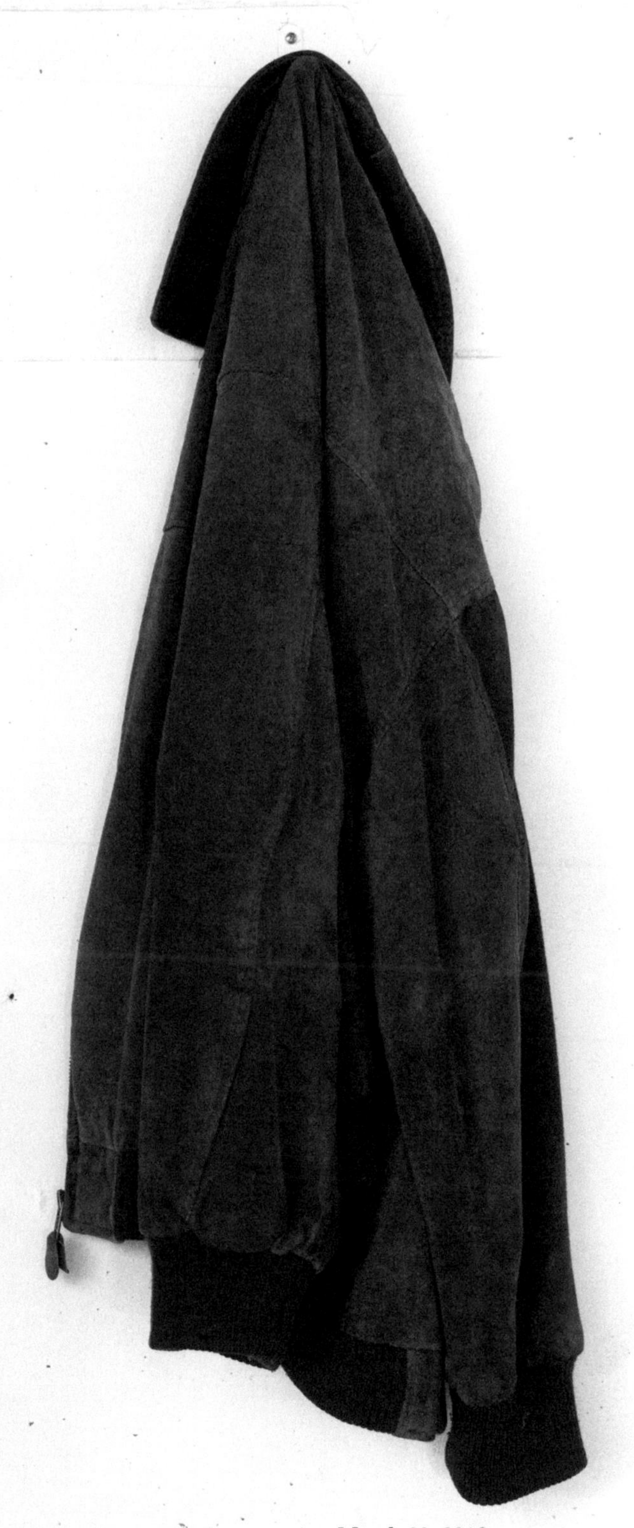

March 29, 2018

Letter to Christian Hofer
Woohi Chung

Hi Christian,

I'm Woohi.

I'm looking forward to seeing you in coming March.
I hope this will be a great opportunity to think about what
is happening today all around the world together. First
I would like to introduce myself briefly and write mainly
about my family history in this letter. I thought it's because
my family history is too long and complicated to talk,
although we can have enough time to talk about ourselves
when we actually meet in Japan. I picked up three repre-
sentative members to share the history; my grandfather on
my mother side, and my aunt and grandmother on my
father side.

Well, I was born in Tokyo, in 1994. Both of my parents
are the second generation of *Zainichi* Korean, so I would be
referred to as the third generation of *Zainichi* Korean. I'm
not sure how much you are familiar with the word *Zainichi*
Korean, I'm describing it quickly just in case. "*Zainichi*"
literally means "living in Japan" and usually indicates Koreans
who came to Japan during the colonial or early post-war
period, and their descendants who were born in Japan. Most
of the first generations of *Zainichi* Koreans were planning
to go back to Korea at first, so they began to build ethnic
schools to teach Korean language to children in many places
in Japan under the severe political oppressions. However,
after recognizing impossibility to make a living in Korean
peninsula where Korean war was on going, those schools
played key roles to nurture Korean identity to live up in
harsh discrimination by Japanese. I am the one of those realized for the first time that I was Korean living in Japan
through attending the elementary school.

February 28, 2018

My grandfather (mother's side) was one *Zainichi* Korean who contributed to maintain the school (where my mom and I also attended). He was born in 1924 meanwhile in colonized Korea. He originally came to Japan due to the conscription, however, he was fortunately not sent to the frontline because Japan was defeated in war in a week since his arrival. I found a star tattoo on his left arm that was inscribed to prevent flight.

Soon after Korea got liberated from Japanese rule in 1945, his sister's couple who lived in Kyoto helped his stay in Japan and he had made money by selling commodities handed by GHQ. A few years later, however, when he attempted to go back to Korea after he succeeded in his business, he lost all his property by fire occurred at the sister's house. Then, he kept to be in Japan and earned money with manufacturing stockings in Fukui, but the factory he owned got collapsed by a huge earthquake in 1948. Then, while he was wondering what to do next, he was deceived by Korean friend calling for fishing net business. I guess he meant those fishing nets as merchandises were stolen by his friend in secret but took them back later, I can't imagine the specific situation though. So, he just attempted to go back to Korea before losing them again, I think he was just an unlucky man; he got a shipwreck caught in a storm on the way stowing away. This event eventually made him to settle in Japan the rest of his life. A few years later, he married with *Zainichi* Korean from Osaka and my mother was born as a second child in Saitama in 1955.

To be honest, it is quite easy (of course not easy!) to fit my mother's side history into the "template" of the *Zainichi* Korean history. For one thing, the ethnic school is one of the big elements to generate "standard" *Zainichi* Korean, as my mom's brothers all spent their young days there and belonged to the community all their lives. On the other hand, it does not mean all of them could afford to attend there and there were a lot of other *Zainichi* Korean who had no other option but to conceal their ethnic roots to survive in Japanese

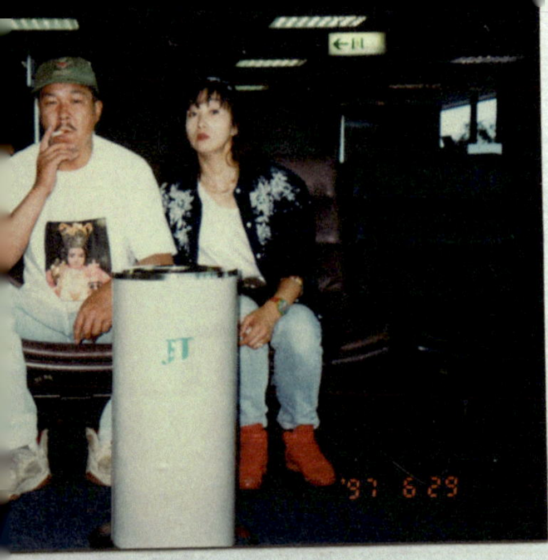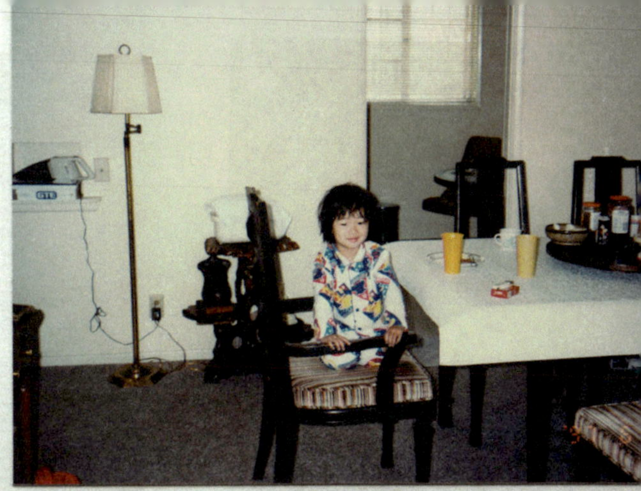

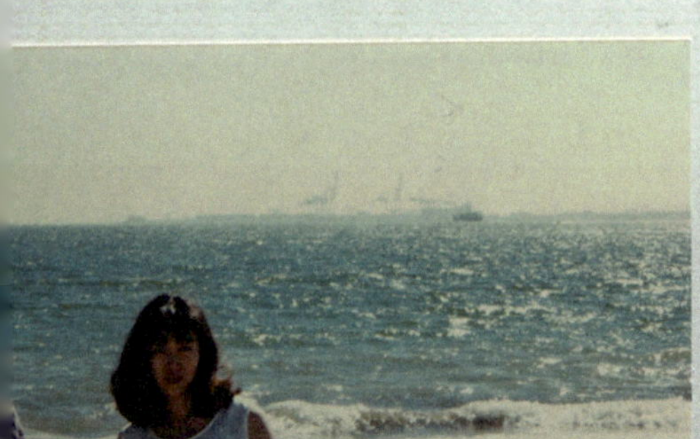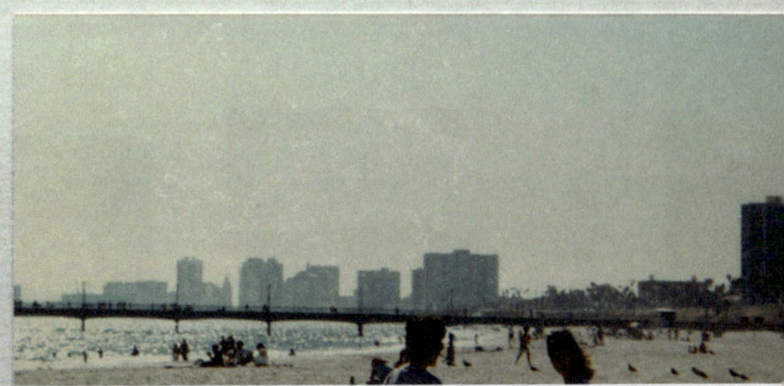

June 29, 1997

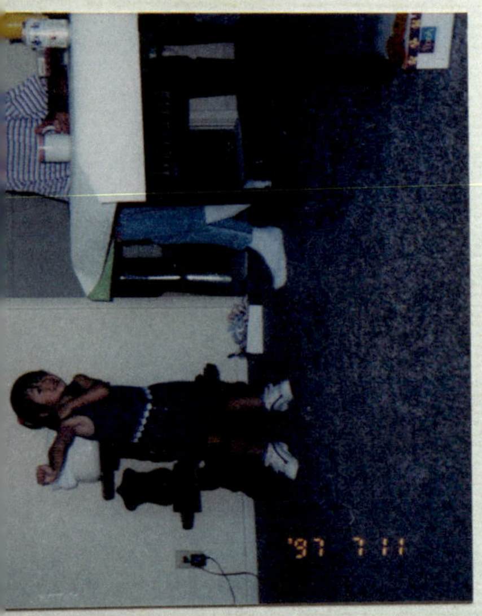

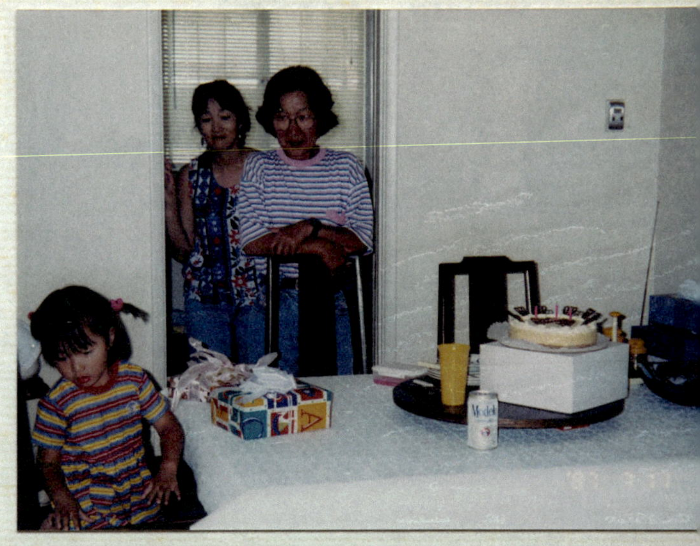

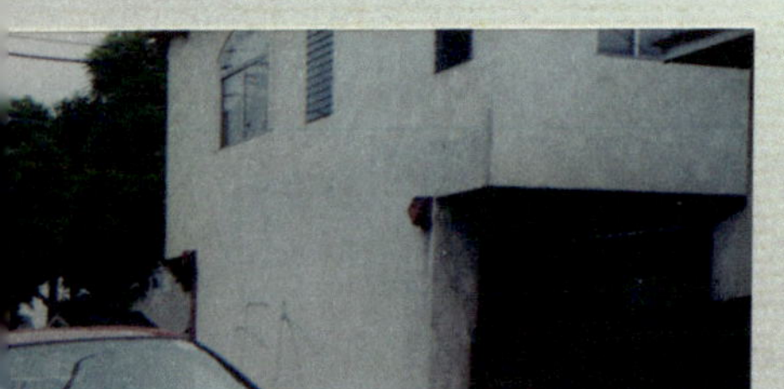

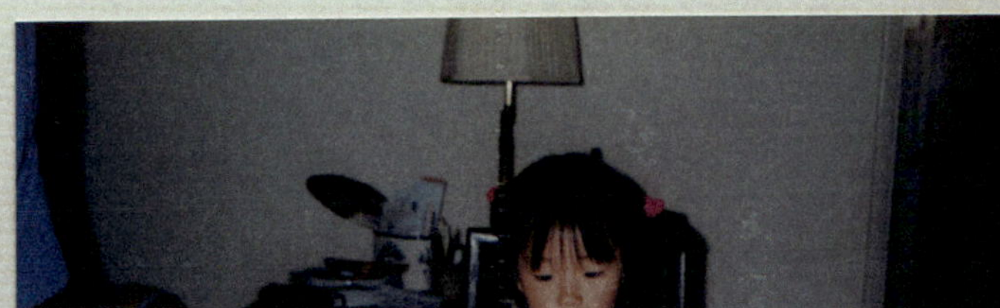

July 11, 1997

society to avoid discrimination. I think my father's side family was one of the examples that distracted from the "main" path of *Zainichi* Korean. For instance, my father just speaks Japanese and uses Japanese name in daily life. According to him, he just attended Japanese schools as a result of objection by his older brothers and sisters who could not agree with the policy of the ethnic school. My father was the youngest among seven siblings but everyone did not get a birth from the same parents. I would like to talk about my grandmother and my aunt, on my father's side history next. When I looked back, the time my aunt and I spent together is clearer than with my grandmother. I have never recognized her as my "grandmother," but it was not weird to think her like that, considering her age.

My aunt, Kiyoko, was born in 1937 in Korea and came to Japan in the very first of the 1940s brought by her mother. Her mother—my grandmother—was on the way chasing her husband who was caught as an arsonist and made a flight to Japan. She met him and had lived together for a few years again, but they finally got divorced due to the domestic violence by her husband. She made a living serving as a maid at Japanese households in the meantime. I have heard that they had experienced Great Tokyo Air Raid in March 1945. Until they had settled in the small Korean village located in the suburb of Tokyo, I imagine they had gone through tremendous struggles in Japanese society. My grandmother used to make money by such as illegal brewing and raising livestock. On the other hand, my aunt went to school carrying her younger sister and brother on her back in the childhood.

When my father was born in 1958—my grandmother at the age of forty-one—my aunt was working at the US base in Sagamihara. She studied English by herself and a friend of her introduced American who was assigned to the military in Japan. She gave birth to a daughter with him and moved to the United States in the late 1960s. However, it was not easy to get a family registration paper that was required for

marriage because she was born in Korea under the colonization. I remember she said to me that she did not know how
many times she tried to give up their marriage. Even if she
found out her relatives in Korea, they treated her abusive
being ashamed of her who marries with American.

Since she was twenty-one years older than my father, he
told me that her role was just like his "mother." While she
was living in the base, my grandmother used to leave him in
her care. I think this experience influenced my father's way
of thinking a lot to foster aspiration for America in his mind.
In my childhood, I often talk to her on the phone or she
sometimes visited us, so I was familiar with her already. The
first time I went to her place by myself in Sacramento,
California, was at the age of twelve, in 2006, and I have visited her and her daughter in Wyoming for several times
using summer vacations since then.

But, please think about it with the current political context; a girl who is attending a Korean ethnic school goes
to America. I realized its weirdness in recent years. I didn't
mention the detail about the ethnic schools before though:
the school organization used to tie with North Korea strongly
from 1960s in the name of federal support to *Zainichi* Korean
(as Japanese government didn't aid them like other normal schools). About forty years later when I entered there in
2001, that organizational energy had already declined, still
I remember that there were portraits of Kim Il-Sung & Kim
Jong-Il in front of the classroom until I was nine year old.
Also, I have another experience that strengthened the abnor-
mality of my life; entering to another Korean school which
is supported by South Korean government in Tokyo for junior-
high and high schools. *Zainichi* Korean who go to the ethnic
school (North Korean side) usually keep belonging to the
same school community or change to Japanese school. So, I
have been struggling with my identity among both Koreas in
Japan, feeling pressure from the United States.

To me, the year of twelve was a big turning point to think
about my identity and I've been through soft identity crisis

constantly so far. I mean, fortunately or not, it did not appear in the form of discrimination by Japanese. Several experiences of visiting America were bitter memories for me because it was almost forced by my father. I just didn't want to leave my home even for a few weeks in summer vacation, and I was so afraid to speak English especially visiting my cousin's place in Wyoming (Kiyoko's daughter, Connie, only speaks English). Her husband and she welcomed me every time, but I think I was not able to answer to their expectation, so I always feel sorry. Also I didn't know how to explain myself. I looked like Japanese but I was not Korean at the same time. The way thinking that I was not Korean was generated during attending (South) Korean school, feeling inferiority to "pure" Korean. (Korean school was like an international school for Koreans from mainland.) I totally lost my own language in America and Korean society. My father never knows.

In the university, I met Cultural Studies, which is a branch derived from sociology, and decided to major in it. I think I was lucky to have such an environment to use my identity academically, not as stigma. For my senior thesis, I wrote about the memory practices of Korean Massacre right after the Great Kantō earthquake in 1923. After I graduated from there last year, I keep studying that field in the master course as well.

Anyway, my three family members I introduced here have all gone today. My grandfather passed away in 2015, my grandmother in 2012, and my aunt in 2014. Maybe I gave you too much information and it may be hard to imagine because our backgrounds are different. But don't worry, their stories are hard to imagine for me as well. I hope this information will be a help for our shooting. See you soon.

Sincerely,

Woohi

February 28, 2018

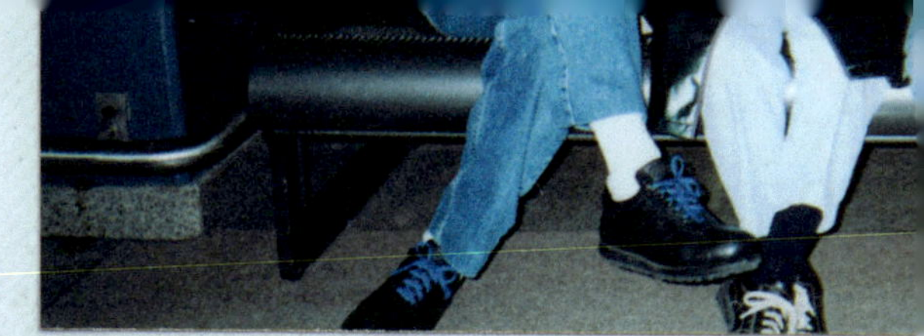

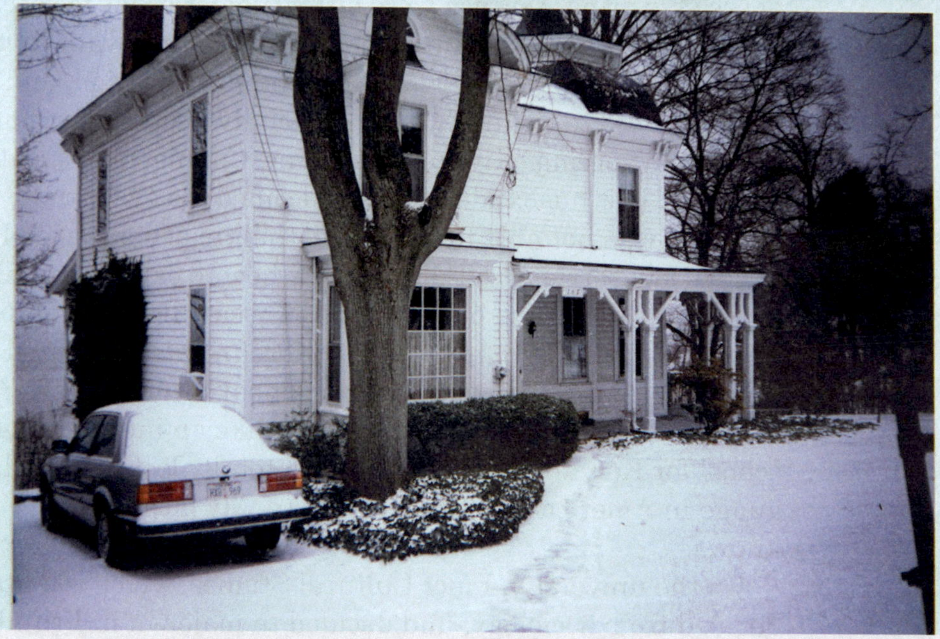

ca. 2000

Letter to Woohi Chung
Christian Hofer

Dear Woohi,

Thank you very much for your letter. I feel honored to learn about your and your family's extraordinary story. I am looking forward to getting to know you.

I am going to tell you the story of my grandparents on my mother's side, as I think it can be seen as a link between us.

Their names are Harumi Komai and Ray Komai. Before they got married my grandmother's maiden name was Kawahara. Both were born in Los Angeles, as so-called Nisei, which is the term for the children of Japanese immigrants. My grandmother was born in 1921 and my grandfather in 1918. At that time there was—and there still is—a large Japanese community in California.

They both grew up in Los Angeles. I don't know too much about their childhood and teenage years, but I will try to give you some insight anyway. They visited regular schools and in addition to that—and by the will of their parents—attended Japanese school in the afternoons, where they were taught Japanese.

They had American friends and were well integrated. I remember my grandfather telling me, that he had felt a lot more American then Japanese. Ray studied design and worked as a typesetter for the family newspaper, the *Rafu Shimpo*, which is a newspaper for the Japanese diaspora in Los Angeles.

My grandmother's father migrated to Canada to work on the construction of the railway system. Later he moved to Los Angeles, where the marriage with Harumi's mother was arranged.

At the time my grandparents met, Harumi was working as a secretary. I do not know exactly how they met, but they both were in their late teens. It was the time before the war which would change their lives and put them into an identity crisis.

Their relationship still was very young when Japan attacked Pearl Harbor and President Roosevelt signed and issued the Executive Order 9066, which allowed the Secretary of War to designate areas inside of the USA to be war zones, which made it possible to incarcerate people based on their ancestry, even if they were US citizens.

All people with a Japanese ancestry living on the West Coast had to sell or give away their properties and were deported to "relocation camps." My grandparents decided to marry, as families were not separated and the period of their imprisonment still was unknown.

My grandmother never liked to talk about that time or how it made her feel. I know that it was a very important and personality defining experience to my grandfather and I think it accompanied him throughout his whole life.

I remember him once telling me that his life had felt normal until Japan attacked the USA and he was imprisoned on behalf of his origin. The incident came unexpected, what made it more shocking as he from one day to the next wasn't viewed anymore as a normal citizen, but as a threat to the country. It also made Ray change the way he saw himself. Suddenly he considered himself also Japanese.

After about six months of imprisonment my grandparents found work away from the West Coast in Chicago, this allowed them to leave the "Relocation Center." After the war, when they were free to move as they pleased, they headed to New York where my mother and my uncle were born. My grandfather managed to start a career as a designer and was hired by different companies and magazines. After a few years, it was 1963, Ray started to work for the US Information Agency, which he liked to call the Cultural CIA. At that time the Information Agency's job was to promote the American culture in different countries, where they had laid foot on and tried to implement the importance of the USA into their collective memory.

March 11, 2018

To me it sounds strange why one would want to work for such an agency and I also can not imagine Ray to be in favor of such an imperialistic idea, as he had very different views. He once told me he had had the feeling he needed to prove that he was a trustworthy American. However my mother believes that my grandmother and grandfather always wanted to visit Japan and that working for the Information Service was a way for them to get there, which in the end worked out—but not as they had expected.

In 1963 they moved from New York to New Delhi where they stayed for five years. Ray was designing exhibitions and publications for the USIS. 1968 when the preparation of the Expo 70 in Osaka began, Ray and Harumi were moved to Japan, so that Ray could coordinate the construction of the US pavilion.

They were very happy about this opportunity and wanted to fully learn Japanese. But as I mentioned, living in Japan did not work out as well as they had hoped for. My grandmother who was raised by her father, because her mother was very ill and died early in her life, only spoke a "masculine farmers" Japanese and also not very well. She didn't realize her Japanese was inappropriate until her Japanese teacher pointed it out. From then on she felt uncomfortable speaking Japanese in public. Ray's Japanese wasn't too good either and had uncomfortable moments as well. A memorable story Ray liked to tell was that they were out on a business dinner and when the group arrived at the lobby, Ray was separated from the group and told that the drivers were seated at another table. In general both my grandparents experienced the behavior of the local Japanese as rather condescending. After some time trying to blend in, they gave up trying to be considered Japanese and started to feel more American again. Nevertheless they stayed in Japan for a few years (until 1973) and accepted that they were not able to fully integrate— they weren't considered either Japanese nor American.

After the Expo they moved from Osaka to Tokyo where my grandfather worked on the design for the USIS (the US

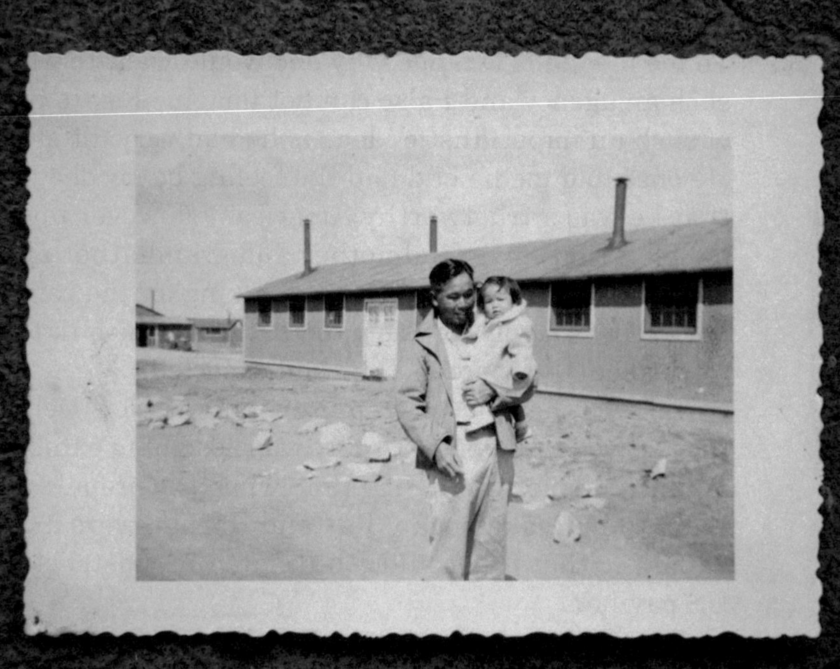

April 15, 1944

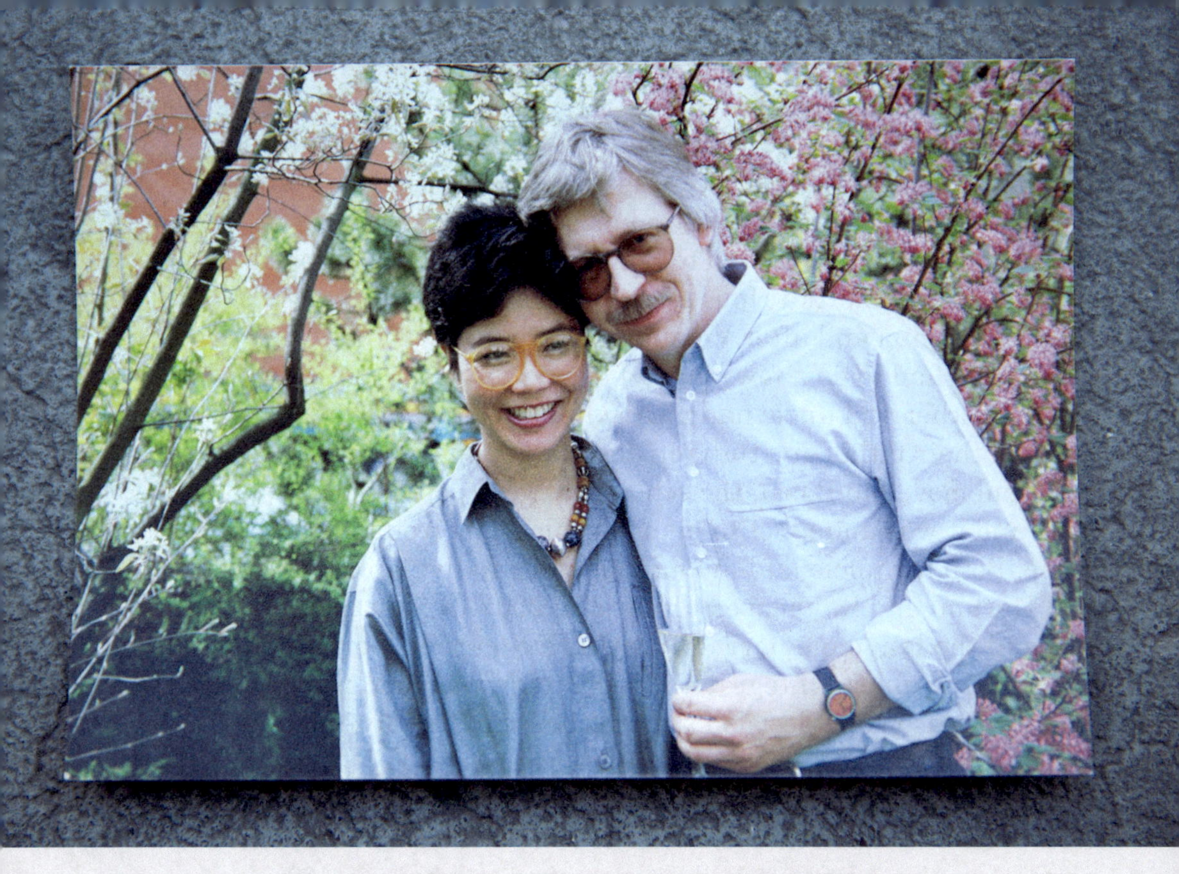

April 27, 1989

Center). I don't know if the building still exists in that state as the US Information Service was dissolved in 1999.

Anyway, his work was viewed as a big success and so Harumi and Ray were moved to Bonn where Ray was stationed to design the "Amerika Houses" in Germany. The next station was Vienna and after Vienna they went back to the USA where Ray had to do a few years of "home service."

My mother and uncle had meanwhile decided to follow the steps of their father in studying design. For their studies they had moved to Basel, the school was very popular at that time and it was a magnet to many people from around the globe. Both my uncle and my mother still are living in Basel and Harumi and Ray moved to Basel in 2007. Due to their age and the language barrier (they never learned German) they weren't able to integrate. Moving to Switzerland was mainly a reasonable decision as both their children lived here. Both of them passed away a few years ago.

To me their story very well shows the dilemma I believe a lot of migrants experience. It seems to be sort of an "in-between state"—you have left but still feel attached to what you left behind. At the same time you settle somewhere new, which doesn't automatically mean that you also have "arrived", in the sense of belonging. They were considered Japanese in the USA, while they were not recognized and accepted as Japanese in Japan. I think it also is a good example of how strongly identities are based upon exclusion and inclusion.

My mother and father met in Basel. My mother was teaching English as a side job and my father, who was working as a chemist, needed to learn some English for his career. My father is Swiss and grew up in the suburbs of Basel. My mother was born in New York and is an American citizen, which also makes me an American on paper. When people here look at me this information is invisible to them, however they see that I have some Asian origin. Although I have these attributes, I never felt American nor Japanese. But thinking about it, I would not define myself either as Swiss. I guess for people in Europe the national identity is not as important as it once was. I think many Europeans including myself do not define themselves that strongly upon where they come from and much more upon what they are interested in, believe in or maybe even through their profession. Growing up in Basel, Germany and France were very close by, I never developed a sense of strict national borders. Throughout my childhood years, before my grandparents moved to Basel, we used to visit them during the summer holidays. After attending school in Basel I moved to Lucerne for my bachelor in graphic design. During my studies in 2011, I spent four months in Leipzig, Germany for an internship. Finishing school I moved to Germany again, to Frankfurt am Main, and worked there for several months in 2013. Following this time in the professional life I decided to do my masters degree and moved to Leipzig again, where I lived until recently. Finishing my studies there I decided to move back to Basel. To me it feels kind of natural to change cities throughout Europe.

I hope I could give you a comprehensible summary of my family's story. I'm looking forward to sharing more thoughts with you throughout the workshop in Tokyo. That might be easier than writing about it.

Kind regards,

Christian

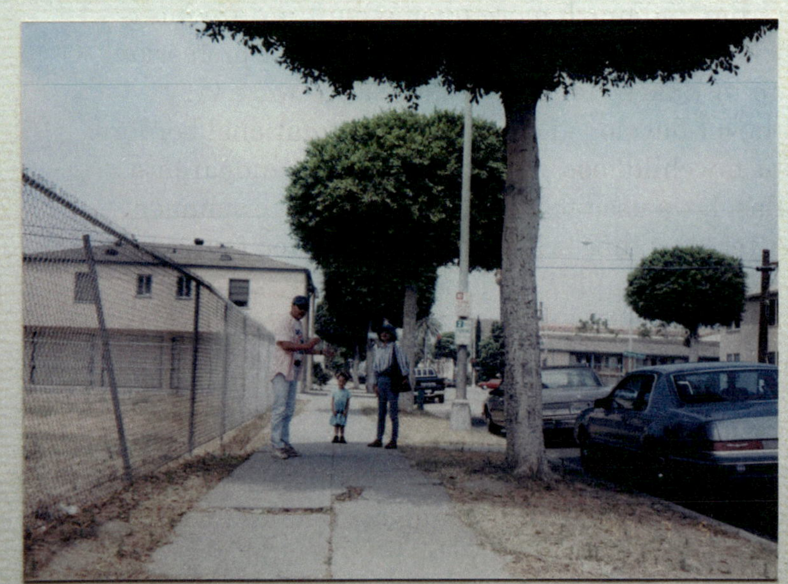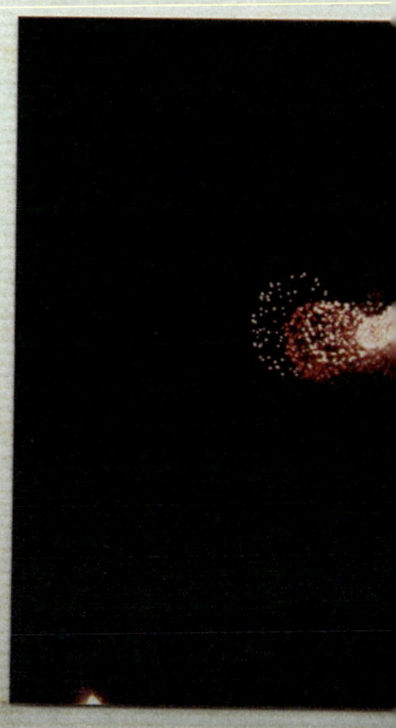

July 5, 1997

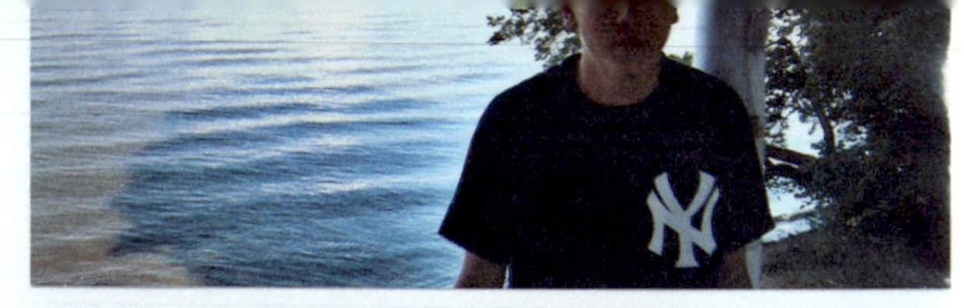

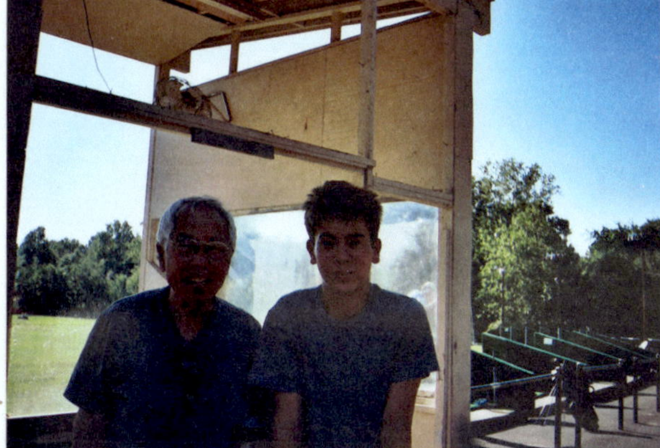

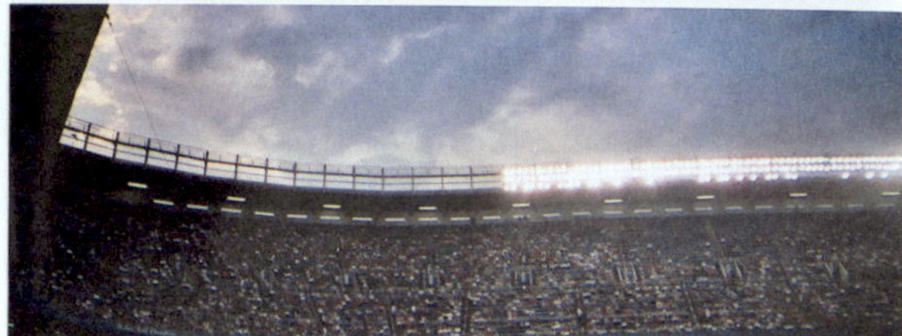

July 2003

A Study of Society in the Mode of Art: On Koki Tanaka's *Vulnerable Histories (A Road Movie)*
Elsa Himmer

It is a phenomenon that can be observed all over the world: public discourses are once again increasingly dominated by voices championing a vision of society based on the demarcation of an in-group and the exclusion of others.[1] Their rhetoric often aims to disparage and vilify individuals or groups of persons and brand them as outsiders to the community. Such defamation causes psychological injuries in those whose membership in society is called in question, and the unstoppable circulation of slurs, in the public sphere and online, can turn the resentments they convey into accepted "knowledge." That is the concern Koki Tanaka harbors with regard to ultra-nationalist groups in his native Japan such as the Zaitokukai. The primary target of their brand of hate speech is the population known as *Zainichi* Koreans: ethnic Koreans whose families have lived in Japan for three or four generations and who grew up and were socialized in Japan; Japanese is the first or even only language for many of them.[2] Responding to this situation, Tanaka's project *Vulnerable Histories (A Road Movie)* (2018) probes the question of how to promote a shared community life grounded in tolerance. The artist stages a multiday

---

1   Examples in Europe include the slogans of the Alternative für Deutschland (AfD) in Germany, the Front National (FN) in France, Fidesz (Hungarian Civic Alliance) in Hungary, and Poland's Prawo i Sprawiedliwość (PiS, Law and Justice). The same characteristics define the rhetoric of President Trump and his advisors as well as the "alt-right" movement in the United States. See Amnesty International, ed., *Amnesty International Report 2017/2018: The State of the World's Human Rights* (London, 2018), 12–14.

2   The label *Zainichi*—which may be translated as "resident in Japan"—describes Koreans whose ancestors came to Japan as voluntary or forced migrants during the colonial period. Many of these families have remained permanent residents in Japan for generations, since Japanese citizenship is hereditary; nationalizations are limited by highly restrictive requirements. See Ludgera Lewerich, "*Zainichi*-Korian: Die koreanische Minderheit in Japan," in *4. Deutsch-japanisch-koreanisches Stipendiatenseminar*, vol. 61 (Berlin: Japanisch-Deutsches Zentrum, 2011), 119–120.

situation in which an extended dialogue unfolds between two protagonists who have not met before: the *Zainichi* Korean woman Woohi Chung and the Swiss national Christian Hofer, whose Japanese grandparents immigrated to the United States around 1900.[3] Many of their interactions and conversations are recorded; their personal histories form the backbone of the films modeled on the movie *Before Sunrise* (1995). Based on Chung's own and her family's story, the film shooting takes the protagonists to various sites in Tokyo that bear special significance for relations between *Zainichi* Koreans and ethnic Japanese and serve as backdrops for their discussion of personal experiences, the social situation in Japan, and the various aspects and potentials of community life more generally.

Building on his own earlier work, Tanaka's *Vulnerable Histories (A Road Movie)* is a study of society in the mode of art, using the example of the *Zainichi* Koreans in Japan to raise questions concerning (cultural) identity, self-perception, and the possibility of tolerant coexistence in the face of the global resurgence of nationalism, populism, and xenophobia. The artist and his camera crew observe as Chung and Hofer test the ways in which personal engagement can foster mutual understanding and a spirit of comity. The following reconstruction of the film production is based on the protagonists' notes in their diaries. The project focuses on the encounter between Chung and Hofer, who entrust each other with their personal recollections and experiences as well as memories handed down in their families. Drawing on these personal narratives, it seeks to render a vivid picture of the pain and insecurity that racist agitation can cause. The encounters between the protagonists reveal existing injuries, but also their willingness to be vulnerable in conversation, to listen to the other and try to understand what moves him or her. From scene to scene, Hofer and Chung alternate in the roles of narrator and listener, contributing their own reflections to extend the conversation beyond the key themes set by Tanaka. The dialogical situations the artist stages for them often begin with personal and, one might think, rather banal questions: favorite dishes, the pleasures of strolling, recreational sports, previous visits to Japan. These trivial subjects illustrate that mutual understanding

3   See the protagonists' letters narrating their family histories, 73–87.

is at issue not only in political debates: it begins in private conversations. Discovering shared experiences and ideas can turn a stranger into a partner and neighbor, someone who is similar to us, with whom we can identify, and such identification is what makes it possible for his fate to concern us. Personal communication, in other words, engenders empathy.[4] This mechanism of rapprochement and understanding is the polar opposite of public agitation. Where racist rhetoric aims to dehumanize individuals or entire groups and establish their alleged otherness as an incontrovertible "fact," the conversations Tanaka stages underscore the protagonists' common humanity. Yet to defeat racist rabble-rousers, Tanaka argues, we need something more than personal dialogue: a public discourse informed by actual knowledge that can minimize fears and the anger and desperation they breed, the racist resentments they fuel. Acquaintance with a multiplicity of diverging perspectives and insight into their agreements as well as disagreements allows us not just to reject the views of radical groups out of empathy with their targets, but also, in the longer view, to expose the fake truths they disseminate as racist constructions. That is why Tanaka arranged for a series of encounters in which light is shed on the social and legal situation of *Zainichi* Koreans and the history they share with the ethnic Japanese population. For example, he invited the *Zainichi* Korean sociologist Tong-hyon Han of the Japan Institute of the Moving Image to give an introductory lecture.[5] As the two protagonists listen, she presents a number of facts that can help refute the racist slogans and accusations and offers an analysis of the shared past of *Zainichi* Koreans and Japanese to suggest how the former might escape the social and legal limbo in which they have long lived.

Adding another voice to the project's dialogical engagement is Nishizaki Masao, a member of the the citizen's organization Housenka, who welcomes the protagonists to the clubhouse on the Arakawa River. With support from *Zainichi* Koreans and Japanese, Housenka works to reconstruct the events around the killings of *Zainichi* Koreans after the

4   See Carolin Emcke, "Das Leid der anderen," *Die Zeit*, no. 52, 2008, http://www.zeit.de/
    2008/52/Mitleid-Essay (accessed April 3, 2018).
5   An abridged version of the lecture is included in the present volume: Tong-hyon Han,
    "*Zainichi* Koreans and Racism in Japan," 101–108.

April 4, 2018

Great Kantō earthquake, which struck the Tokyo region in 1923. The tremors caused widespread disruptions, large fires broke out, and the authorities declared a state of emergency. An orchestrated smear campaign—the association's research revealed the leading part played by a government-controlled radio station—blamed the Korean community for the chaos. Citizens formed militias that subsequently, like the military, conducted targeted executions of Koreans; the victims were hastily buried in a mass grave by the Arakawa. In the public discourse in Japan, however, this reconstruction of what happened remains highly contentious.[6] To preserve the memory of the victims and encourage public discussion, Housenka erected a memorial on its private premises that commemorates the *Zainichi* Koreans who were killed in the massacres. The association's work is an exemplary reminder of the importance of open dialogue, be it about the past or the present situation, a frank engagement involving a multiplicity of voices in which different and contradictory perspectives are reconciled; this polyphony helps replace schematic divisions into good and evil, right and wrong, with a multifaceted representation of society in all its complexity. At the same time, revisiting history helps pave the way for a better mutual understanding in conversation: generating awareness of the past and the origins of today's conflicts, it allows for a recognition of the psychological and physical suffering that has been inflicted and reveals that many of the heated debates of the present grow out of old wounds that have festered because no one took responsibility, the instigators of past crimes were never identified, and no apology was ever offered. Yet all community life is grounded in respect for the rights and dignity of each individual, as Tanaka suggests, asking the

6   In 2016, a citizens' initiative protested a monument in Tokyo's Metropolitan Yokoamicho Park dedicated to the Koreans who died during the earthquake. They took offense at the inscription, which also commemorates the ca. 6,000 Koreans killed after the earthquake. The initiative argued that it was unacceptable to inculcate this version of the events in Japanese children's minds. Around the same time, the Tokyo municipal administration declared that it would no longer send a letter of condolence to the annual commemorative event held on the earthquake's anniversary. See Narusawa Muneo, "Behind Tokyo Governor Koike's Refusal to Send a Eulogy to the 'Memorial Service for Korean Victims of the Great Kantō-Earthquake': A Rightist Women's Group and Nippon Kaigi," trans. Satoko Oka Norimatsu, *The Asia-Pacific-Journal* 15, issue 24, no. 5 (2017): 4–5.

protagonists, by the Arakawa, to read from the Universal Declaration of Human Rights: "All human beings are born free and equal in dignity and rights. They are endowed with reason and conscience and should act towards one another in a spirit of brotherhood."[7]

Laws and international treaties are overarching sets of rules designed to control human behavior and provide the legal framework for a community life based on humanist values. The significance of legal protections for interactions between people is another aspect that *Vulnerable Histories (A Road Movie)* spotlights. At a playground in Fujimi Park, where nationalists shouting hate-filled slogans often begin their marches, the protagonists read article 4 of the United Nations' International Convention on the Elimination of All Forms of Racial Discrimination. It enjoins legislatures to criminalize such discrimination, ethnic hatred, and any incitement to violence. Japan ratified the convention in 1995 but entered a reservation that it would fulfill the obligations under said article only to the extent compatible with the rights to freedom of assembly, association, and expression.[8] So how to ban hate speech, or at least contain its power to wound, when racists invoke their right to assembly and expression? Banning slogans only relieves the symptoms when the mechanisms that drive people to shout them remain unaddressed. One section of *Vulnerable Histories (A Road Movie)* accordingly consists of the two protagonists sitting down to review YouTube videos documenting the nationalists' marches. Such reenactment of the trauma caused by hate-filled rhetoric would seem to be indispensable: repeating vilifying speech in a different context can be a way to attempt to break the cycle of injury and victimization.[9] The films effect this recontextualization also through the knowledge shared by Tong-hyon Han in her lecture and by Nishizaki Masao in presenting the work of the Korean-Japanese history association. Contrasting it with the videos of the rallies brings home that

7   Universal Declaration of Human Rights (1948), http://www.ohchr.org/EN/UDHR/
     Documents/UDHR_Translations/eng.pdf (accessed April 3, 2018).
8   See 2nd International Convention on the Elimination of All Forms of Racial Discrimination,
     New York (1966), https://treaties.un.org/Pages/ViewDetails.aspx?src=IND&mtdsg_
     no=IV-2&chapter=4&lang=en (accessed April 3, 2018).
9   See Judith Butler, *Excitable Speech: A Politics of the Performative* (New York: Routledge,
     1997), 37–38.

the alleged facts the Zaitokukai and other groups muster to support their calumnies are nothing but racist constructions.

The scenarios Tanaka designs produce moments of understanding that can defuse the racist rallying cries poisoning social life. Emphasizing personal dialogue, they highlight that taking a stand for tolerant coexistence is everyone's responsibility. The artist makes the case that we all can and should offer opposition to nationalism, populism, and xenophobia. Needless to say, he does not prompt us to seek out violent confrontations or insist on equally radical opposite standpoints; on the contrary, he encourages us to ask critical questions about social realities and keep an open mind. The need to do so is the subject of a core scene of the project, the single longest conversation, conducted, in an allusion to the subtitle, *A Road Movie*, in a car. The characters do not go on a literal road trip—the car and passengers are in a well-lit gallery space—but are companions on a symbolic voyage of emotional exploration. The question of the possibility of community is ultimately a very personal one, to be negotiated between individuals. In Tanaka's project, the trajectory of this voyage weaves between documentation and fiction: the artist has arranged the encounter between the two protagonists, prepared cues for their conversations, and made appointments with various experts from whom they learn more. No effort is made to conceal this theatrical aspect: when Chung and Hofer operate the camera equipment, their double role becomes conspicuous—they contribute their personal histories and experiences to the project, but they are also actors inside a setting determined by the artist. Now and then, Tanaka's voice can be heard offscreen, signaling his involvement as the "mastermind" behind the experiment, until, toward the end, he reveals himself by stepping in front of the camera.

Based on simplifications and selective ignorance, the worldviews proffered by racists divide societies into hostile camps. *Vulnerable Histories (A Road Movie)*, by contrast, puts the emphasis on dialogue. Tanaka reminds us of the dangers of ceding control over the interpretation of reality to small but vocal groups who pass off a myopic worldview as the truth and simplistic narratives as history. If they are left unchecked, they may in the long run undermine the life of communities founded on humanist values, in Japan, but also in Europe, where nationalist-populist parties are on the rise, or in the United States, where the "alt-right" movement has revived the notion that society is defined by a clash between members and outsiders. Dialogue—in the form of private conversations as well as public discourse—is crucial, the artist proposes, if we are to take a stand against forces of inequality and injustice that increasingly threaten to contaminate our speech and disfigure our shared life. It is the only way to bridge the widening gulfs of enmity between different factions, balance and reconcile diverging opinions, and enlist support for the ongoing quest to build a life of mutual respect and tolerance in which we learn about each other instead of clinging to resentful stereotypes.

April 4, 2018

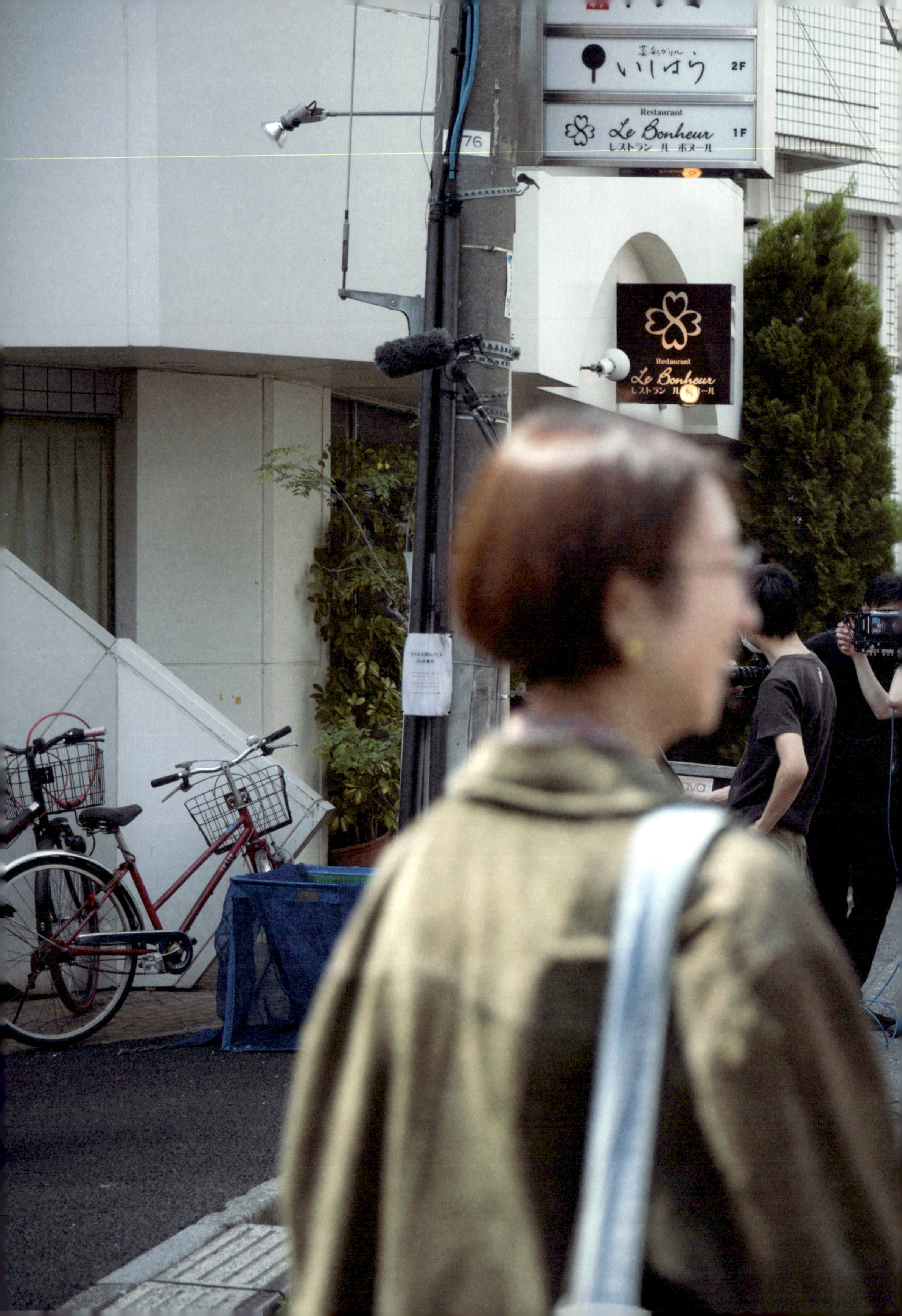
菜彩グリル
いしはら 2F
Restaurant
Le Bonheur 1F
レストラン ル ボヌール
Restaurant
Le Bonheur
レストラン ル ボヌール
76

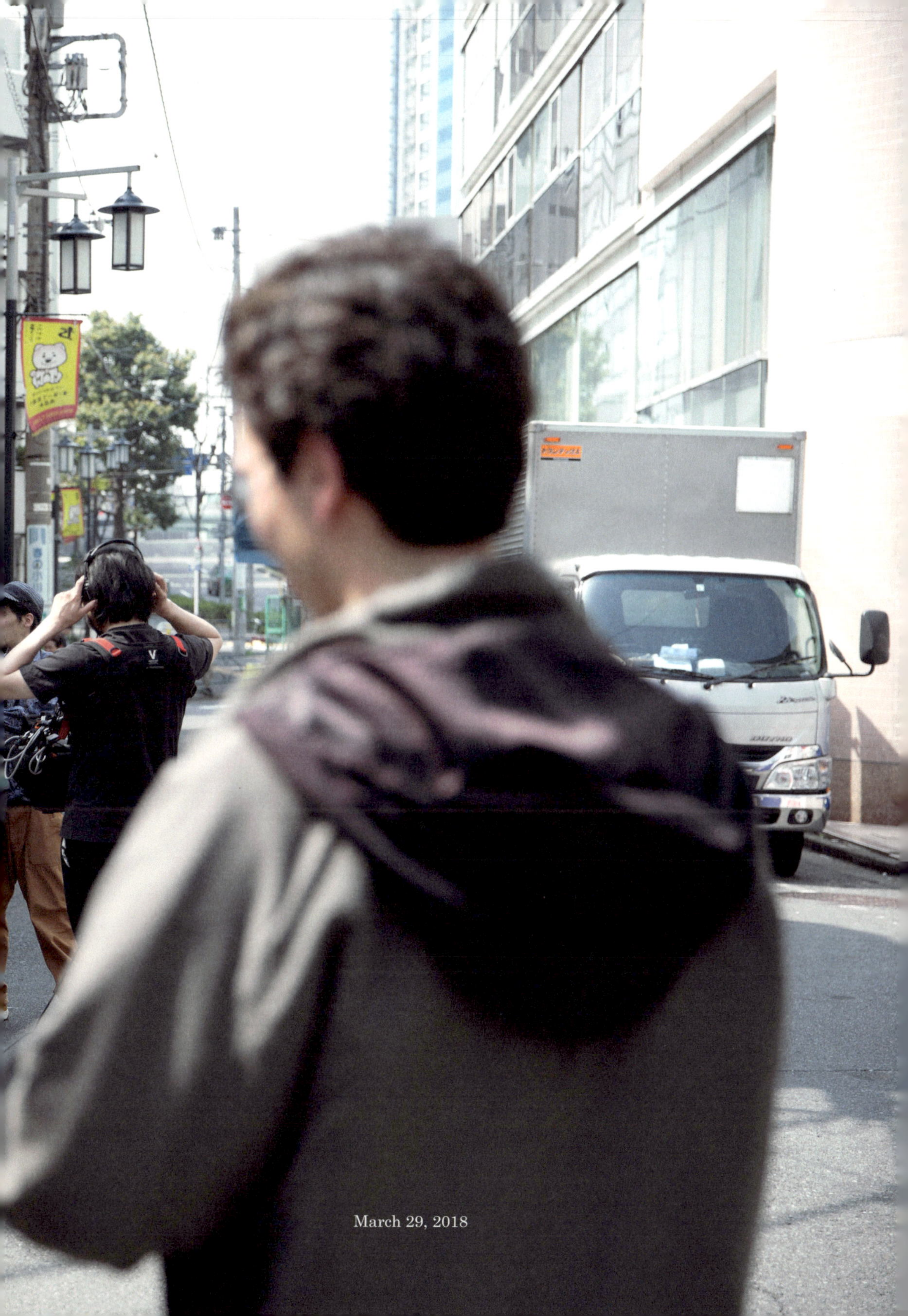

March 29, 2018

I think I should explain the thinking behind the commissioning of the following text. One thing that has struck me when I've worked on projects in Europe in recent years is how nationalism—and the racism and xenophobia against Muslim immigrants associated with it—is such a widespread issue there. Under the Trump administration, similar problems have become more pronounced in the United States too. But of course every place has its own situation, and anti-immigrant sentiment is not necessarily directed at Muslims only. So what is it like in Asia, or Japan?

I lived in Los Angeles from 2009 to 2016. On my visits home during that time, I would come across marches by people brandishing national flags, and see news reports about incidents of hate speech targeting Korean residents of Japan (*Zainichi* Koreans). Once, in Kawasaki, I even saw a group of people returning from a march who shouted horrible things as they walked through the station. To me, this shows how the specific contexts of racism appear in tandem with the global form of racism.

The author of the following text, the sociologist Tong-hyon Han, was one of the six participants in my previous project, *Possibilities for being together. Their praxis*, presented at Art Tower Mito in 2016. She is also a *Zainichi* Korean. I asked her to participate in the current project as an advisor and facilitator. The text is based on a talk she gave at a preliminary study session for the cast and crew members at the start of the project.

Meeting Tong-hyon Han was an important event for me. In Japan, I am ultimately a member of the majority of "Japanese" people. I inevitably see things from the perspective of the majority. But my conversations with Tong-hyon Han led me to critically reassess my position. On the other hand, when I am in Europe and the United States, I become a member of the "Asian" minority. The awareness of racism that I gained from these shifts in perspective is the starting point for this project.

How can the problems faced by *Zainichi* Koreans in Japan be positioned in the global context of racism? My approach to addressing this question may be abstract, but nevertheless I feel some minimal context is necessary for viewers to understand the work. This is why I asked Tong-hyon Han to write an overview of the situation.

Koki Tanaka

January 19, 2018

Zainichi Koreans and Racism in Japan
Tong-hyon Han

Broadly defined, the term "*Zainichi* Korean" refers to the ethnic Koreans who emigrated to Japan as a result of the Japanese colonization of Korea, as well as their descendants.

Colonial Rule and Korean Migration to Japan

Japan annexed the Korean Peninsula in 1910. From then on, Korea was a Japanese colony, and its people were Japanese imperial subjects. But with the implementation of the Korean Family Registry Ordinance, the Koreans were completely excluded from the *koseki* or family registry law that formed the basis for establishing legal personhood in Japan.

Whereas the domain of the Japanese empire at the promulgation of the Constitution of the Great Empire of Japan (the Meiji Constitution) in 1890 was considered the "homeland," newly acquired lands were designated "overseas territories" to which the constitution did not apply. That is, even as it absorbed the Korean people as imperial subjects and adopted a policy of cultural assimilation, the colonial administration still enforced a difference in status by means of a separate family registry system. What made this distinction possible was the racist belief that the subjugated people were necessarily inferior to the superior ruling people.

There were 790 Koreans in Japan in 1909, the year before the annexation, but by the end of World War II in 1945, that number had risen to 2.3 million, or about one-tenth of the total Korean population at the time. Since life was hard in Korea under the colonial regime, in the early years most Koreans came to Japan looking for better living conditions. Later, in response to acute labor shortages due to the escalation of war in the Asia-Pacific from the late 1930s onward, there were more cases of conscripted or semi-conscripted labor migration.

January 28, 2018

Most of these migrants repatriated after the defeat of Japan and liberation of Korea in August 1945—but there were quite a few who delayed their return because of the uncertainty of the political situation in the Korean Peninsula, or because they had already established livelihoods in Japan. There were between five and six hundred thousand such people in 1947, and then, with the outbreak of the Korean War in 1950, the way home grew even more difficult. This is the origin of the *Zainichi* Koreans.

Exclusion by Means of Revoked Nationality

Based on the interpretation that they were still foreigners even though they had been Japanese subjects since the colonial era, in May 1947 the Japanese government under Allied occupation declared that the Koreans who remained in Japan would be subject to an Alien Registration Ordinance, implemented the day before the enforcement of the postwar constitution. But since a successor state had yet to be established on the Korean Peninsula, the nationality of such people was registered as *Chōsen*,[1] in a continuation of the colonial-era extraterritorial registry system.

The *Zainichi* Koreans were treated arbitrarily by the Allies and the Japanese government for the rest of the occupation: registered as foreigners and put under strict control, they were nevertheless forced to shut down the ethnic schools they had built for themselves, which were deemed unlawful on the grounds that as Japanese subjects the Koreans should comply with compulsory education.

The Allied occupation of Japan came to an end with the enforcement of the San Francisco Peace Treaty in April 1952. Immediately prior, the Japanese government unilaterally revoked the Japanese nationality of all former colonial subjects. Although their legal status was undefined, *Zainichi* Koreans were granted tacit approval to remain in Japan—but they were also subjected to an Immigration Control Ordinance that included provisions for deportation. At the same time, since Japanese nationality was a requirement for drawing military pensions and other

1   Derived from the Chinese characters used in the name of the Joseon dynasty (1392–
     1897), *Chōsen* is the historical Japanese name for Korea, and the name applied to the
     Korean colony by the colonial administration.—Trans.

January 28, 2018

forms of social support (during the colonial period a significant number of Koreans had been sent to battle as soldiers and staff of the Japanese army), *Zainichi* Koreans were also denied access to a wide range of public welfare programs.

In this way, *Zainichi* Koreans were systematically excluded from Japanese society as mere foreigners with no connection to Japan. On top of which, they were "foreigners" without a nationality to replace their Japanese citizenship: being a *Chōsen* national was equivalent to being a stateless "alien."

Nationality and Residency Status

The governments of Japan and the Republic of Korea (South Korea) began negotiations about normalizing relations after the enforcement of the San Francisco Peace Treaty, concluding the Treaty on Basic Relations Between Japan and the Republic of Korea in 1965. According to the treaty's agreement on legal status, *Zainichi* Koreans who changed their nationality from *Chōsen* to "South Korea" (possible since 1950) were granted "treaty-based permanent residency" status.

On the other hand, the legal status of those who kept their *Chōsen* nationality remained unresolved. With the normalization of Japan–Korea relations, "South Korea" was recognized as an actual nationality in the Japanese alien registration system, while *Chōsen* was now nothing but a place-name or empty signifier. Yet there was a time after the war when many Koreans in Japan supported the Democratic People's Republic of Korea (North Korea) as their homeland, and since North Korea extended aid to such *Zainichi* Koreans—in particular for the educational programs at the *Chōsen* schools that had been suppressed and then rebuilt[2]—not a few of those who kept their *Chōsen* nationality instead of switching to South Korea felt sympathy for and even a degree of attachment to North Korea.

2   Although often translated as "Korean school," the term *Chōsen gakkō* refers specifically to the pro–North Korea schools affiliated with the General Association of Korean Residents in Japan (Chongryon). These schools should not be confused with the schools supported by South Korea and operated by the Korean Residents Union in Japan (Mindan), referred to in Japanese as *Kankoku gakkō*.—Trans.

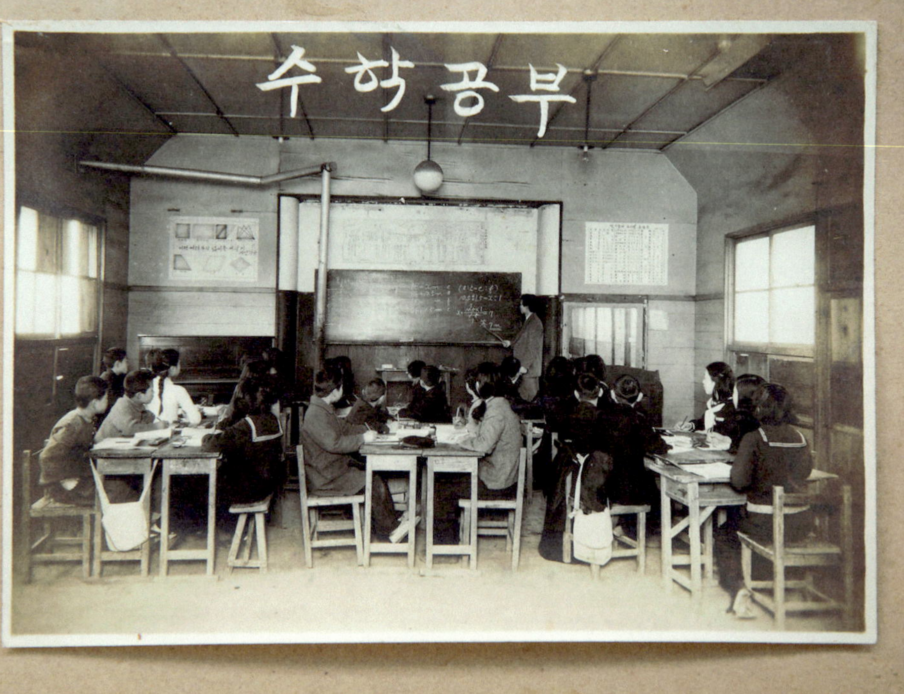

1950

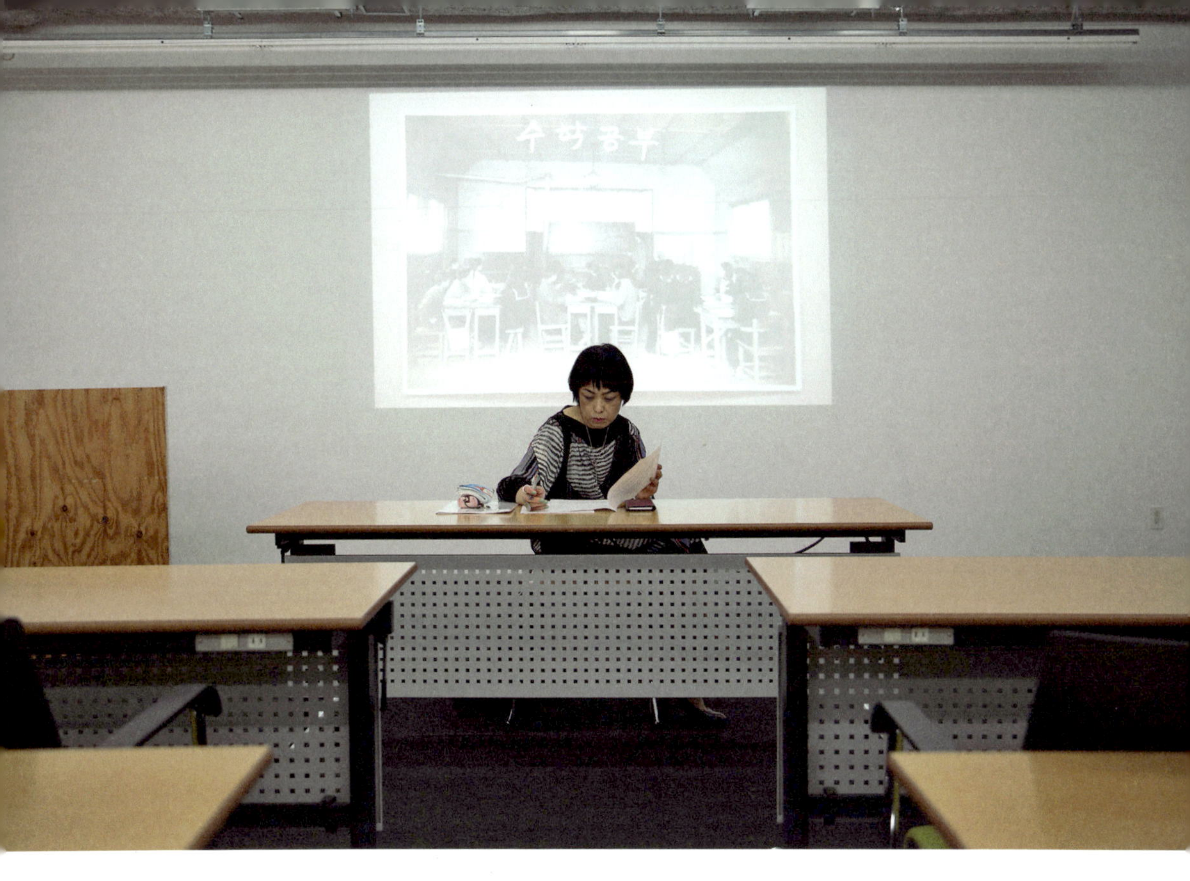

April 1, 2018

Then, with the Japanese adoption of the United Nations Protocol Relating to the Status of Refugees in 1982, and the elimination of nationality as a condition for receiving social security benefits, the *Chōsen* registrants (stateless Koreans) were also granted the status of "exceptional permanent residents." Finally, upon the finalization of a memorandum between the foreign ministers of Japan and South Korea in 1991, the "treaty-based permanent residency" and "exceptional permanent residency" statuses were streamlined into the "special permanent residency" status, which was automatically conferred upon all *Zainichi* Koreans, including those from the third generation on. Currently, there are about 330,000 *Zainichi* Korean special permanent residents in Japan who acquired their residency in this way.

Now, what requires special attention here is the Japanese citizenship system. Japanese nationality law is based on consanguinity. In other words, a second-generation immigrant born in Japan must take the nationality of his or her parents, with no exceptions made even for former colonial subjects. As such, unless they naturalize, immigrants in Japan are institutionally defined as foreigners, irrespective of how many generations they may have actually lived there. There is a strong sense among Japanese that those of foreign lineage are outsiders. Moreover, naturalization involves a cumbersome process that requires applicants to compile a dauntingly high amount of paperwork and documentation. We could even say this is typical of Japanese society, which conflates nationality, lineage, and culture, and tends to view Japanese and foreigners in binary terms.

And yet the number of *Zainichi* Koreans who choose to naturalize increases each year. In addition to the above-mentioned special permanent residents, there are those who obtain Japanese citizenship through naturalization (a cumulative total of some 360,000 since 1952), as well as those with a Japanese parent who choose to become Japanese citizens (over eighty percent of the *Zainichi* Koreans who married in 2012 had a Japanese spouse, and there are some five thousand children born to such families who are allowed to hold dual citizenship until the age of twenty-two, when under current law they must choose between the two nationalities). To the extent that they share the same historical background, all of the above can be called *Zainichi* Koreans.

January 28, 2018

Hate Speech and Its Targets

The *Zainichi* Koreans were brought to Japan in part by a historical process that began with the colonial period and its cultural assimilation policies. Economically and culturally, they are now fully integrated into Japanese society.

Even so, they have suffered from discrimination that originates at the interpersonal level from the former ideology of colonialism, and on the institutional level from the nationality barrier that was set up when Japan abandoned its responsibility as a former imperial power. Entering the twenty-first century, there has been minimal progress toward multiculturalism either institutionally or in terms of broader social awareness, and *Zainichi* Koreans are now confronting a surge in xenophobia and racism that seems to have arisen out of a pervasive sense of social malaise in Japanese society on the one hand, and in reaction to self-made advances in social standing by *Zainichi* Koreans on the other.

Reinforcing the government's nationality barrier, racists view the *Zainichi* Koreans not as members of the same society, but as foreign outsiders who are still loyal to another homeland. As a result, *Zainichi* Koreans are exposed to spikes in hate speech whenever any kind of diplomatic conflict occurs between Japan and South or North Korea, and now the racist abuse has become routine.

Forgetting entirely about the historical circumstances, Japanese racists attack the "privileges" of permanent residency status and access to social security granted to *Zainichi* Koreans, even though these are in fact their minimum rights. At first expressions of hatred were prominent in online communities, but after a racist group attacked a *Chōsen* school in Kyoto in 2009, demonstrations by people shouting racist slogans as they marched through *Zainichi* Korean neighborhoods became a common occurrence.

Since to that point Japan did not have any laws prohibiting hate speech and hate crimes, such marches were carried out legally, and they became a social problem. In response, a citizen-led countermovement successfully lobbied for a law to eliminate hate speech, The Act on the Promotion of Efforts to Eliminate Unfair Discriminatory Speech and Behavior against Persons Originating from Outside Japan, passed in 2016. But lacking prohibitions and penalties, the law is essentially a statement of principle only, and since it is highly specific to acts of hate speech against people with foreign roots who are legally residing in Japan, there is much work left to be done.

At present the Japanese government has shown little indication of pursuing further countermeasures. But Japan's abandonment of its responsibility as a former imperial power in 1952, when it cut off its former colonial subjects as foreigners with no connection to the country and stripped them of their rights, could itself be called an institutionalization of racism based on the pretext of nationality in the first place.

This is exemplified in the treatment of the *Chōsen* schools that the *Zainichi* Koreans rebuilt on their own in the 1950s and 1960s and then ran with aid from North Korea. Refusing to recognize them as regular schools, the Japanese government has never provided the *Chōsen* schools with any material support, assistance, or accreditation. Such schools qualify for the "High School Tuition Waiver Program" that was initiated in 2010, which applies to foreign-run and international schools, but they have been excluded from the program without legal basis because of diplomatic issues with North Korea over nuclear testing and the abduction of Japanese citizens.

Arguing that this policy is discriminatory, several *Chōsen* schools are now suing the Japanese government in court.

January 28, 2018

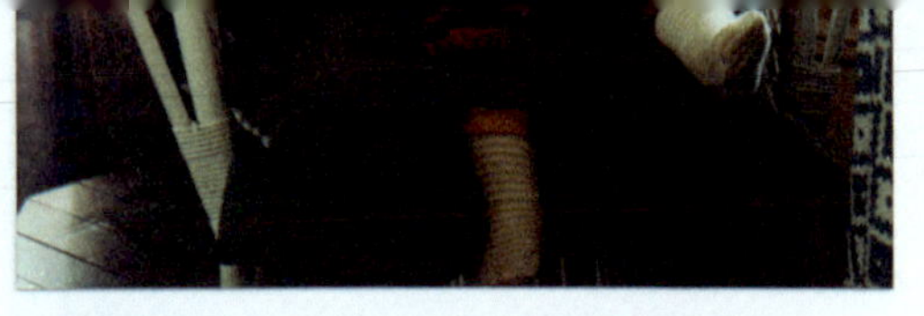
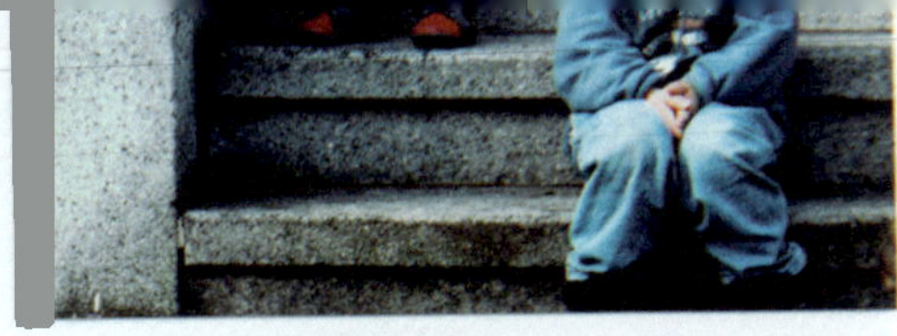
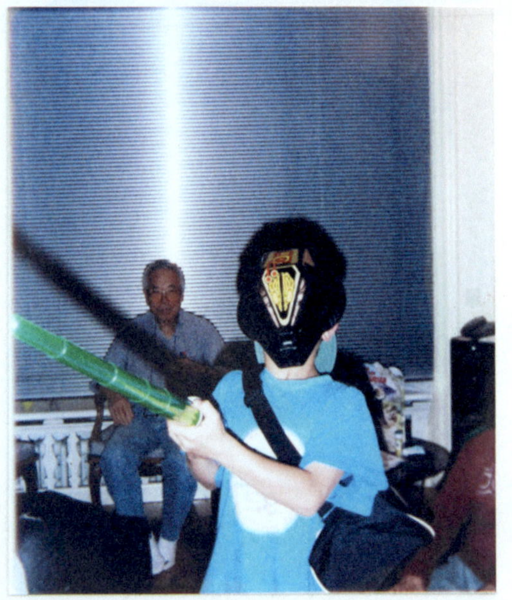
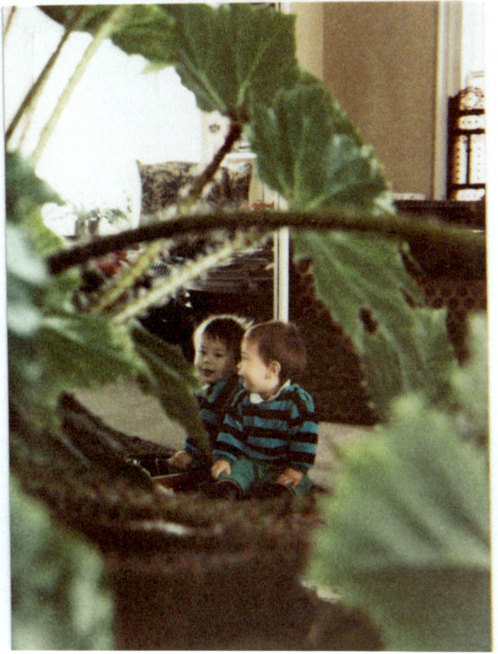

1998 / April 1990

KOKI TANAKA

Born 1975 in Tochigi, Japan
Lives and works in Kyoto

EDUCATION

2005
MA Fine Arts, Tokyo University of the Arts

2000
BA Fine Arts, Tokyo Zokei University

AWARDS

2015
Artist of the Year, Deutsche Bank

2013
Special Mention (National Participation),
Venice Biennale

SELECTED SOLO EXHIBITIONS (SINCE 2004)

2018
*Koki Tanaka: Vulnerable Histories
(A Road Movie)*, Migros Museum für
Gegenwartskunst, Zurich

2017
Provisional Studies (Working Title), Kunsthaus
Graz
La Permanence, Villa Vassilieff, Paris

2016
*Provisional Studies – Action #5: Conceiving
the Past, Perceiving the Present*,
The Showroom, London
Possibilities for being together. Their praxis,
Art Tower Mito
Poet and Potter, Asian Art Museum, San
Francisco

2015
A Vulnerable Narrator, Deferred Rhythms,
Museo d'Arte Contemporanea, Rome
A Vulnerable Narrator, Deutsche Bank
KunstHalle, Berlin

2014
*A Piano Played by Five Pianists at Once
(First Attempt)*, Passerelle – Centre d'art
contemporain, Brest

2013
Japanese Pavilion, Venice Biennale

2012
*A Piano Played by Five Pianists at Once
(First Attempt)*, Room Gallery, University
of California, Irvine

SELECTED GROUP EXHIBITIONS (SINCE 2006)

2011
In a Place Between Snow Balls and Stones,
 Aoyama Meguro, Tokyo
Dog, Bus, Palm Tree, The Box, Los Angeles

2010
*Nothing Related, but Something Could Be
 Associated*, Yerba Buena Center for the
 Arts, San Francisco
Random Hours, YYZ Artist's Outlet, Toronto

2009
On a Day to Day Basis, Vitamin Creative
 Space, Guangzhou
Simple Gesture and Temporary Sculpture,
 Aoyama Meguro, Tokyo

2008
*Here Shows Recent Works in New Installations,
 by the Way*, Museum of Modern Art,
 Gunma, Takasaki
The End of the Summer: New Paintings,
 Aoyama Meguro, Tokyo

2007
Turning the Lights On, Centre A, Vancouver
Sound Test, stc, NADiff, Tokyo
Everything Is Everything, Hiroshima City
 Museum of Contemporary Art
Past, Present, Future, Ueno Royal Museum,
 Tokyo
Setting up and Taking down, Module, Palais
 de Tokyo, Paris

2005
Save the World!, Aoyama Meguro, Tokyo

2004
Kakusei in the Air, Aoyama Meguro, Tokyo
Plastic Bags, Beer, Caviar to Pigeons, etc.,
 Museum of Modern Art, Gunma,
 Takasaki
All About All the Nights, Gallery Caption, Gifu

2017
Venice Biennale
Skulptur Projekte Münster
Action!, Kunsthaus Zürich
*Reenacting History – Collective Actions and
 Everyday Gestures*, National Museum
 of Modern and Contemporary Art,
 Gwacheon
L'Alternative, FRAC Champagne-Ardenne,
 Reims
*Propositions for Non-Fascist Living,
 "Propositions #1: What We Mean*, basis
 voor actuele kunst, Utrecht
JAPANORAMA, Centre Pompidou Metz

2016
Liverpool Biennial
Ensemble sin órganos, Centro de Arte
 Contemporáneo Wifredo Lam, Havana
Tell Me a Story: Locality and Narrative,
 Rockbund Art Museum, Shanghai

2015
*Parasophia: Kyoto International Festival of
 Contemporary Culture*, Kyoto Municipal
 Museum of Art

2014
Positions, Van Abbemuseum, Eindhoven
Journal, ICA, London
Play Time, Les Ateliers de Rennes – biennale
 d'art contemporain
*The Part In The Story Where A Part Becomes
 A Part Of Something Else*, Witte de With,
 Rotterdam

2013
*Reading Cinema, Finding Words: Art after
 Marcel Broodthaers*, National Museum
 of Modern Art, Kyoto; National
 Museum of Modern Art, Tokyo

112

Unknown Forces, Tophane i Amire Culture
	and Arts Center, Istanbul
California-Pacific Triennial, Orange County
	Museum of Art, Newport Beach

2012
Made in L.A., Hammer Museum, Los Angeles
Ça & là, Fondation d'entreprise Ricard, Paris
Sensory Training, Vitamin Creative Space,
	Guangzhou
Trading Futures, Taipei Contemporary Art
	Center

2011
Yokohama Triennale
Making Is Thinking, Witte de With,
	Rotterdam

2010
A Rock That Was Taught It Was A Bird,
	Artspace, Auckland

2009
The View From Elsewhere, Sherman
	Contemporary Art Foundation, Sydney

2008
Gwangju Biennale
Busan Biennale
*Platform Seoul 2008: I have nothing to say
	and I am saying it*, Samuso, Seoul

2007
Re-trait, Fondation d'entreprise Ricard, Paris
*All about Laughter: Humor in Contemporary
	Art*, Mori Art Museum, Tokyo
*Living in the Material World. Things in Art of
	the 20th Century and Beyond*, National
	Art Center, Tokyo
The Door into Summer: The Age of Micropop,
	Art Tower Mito

2006
Taipei Biennale
Echigo-Tsumari Art Triennial 2006, Niigata
Le Cabane, Palais de Tokyo, Paris

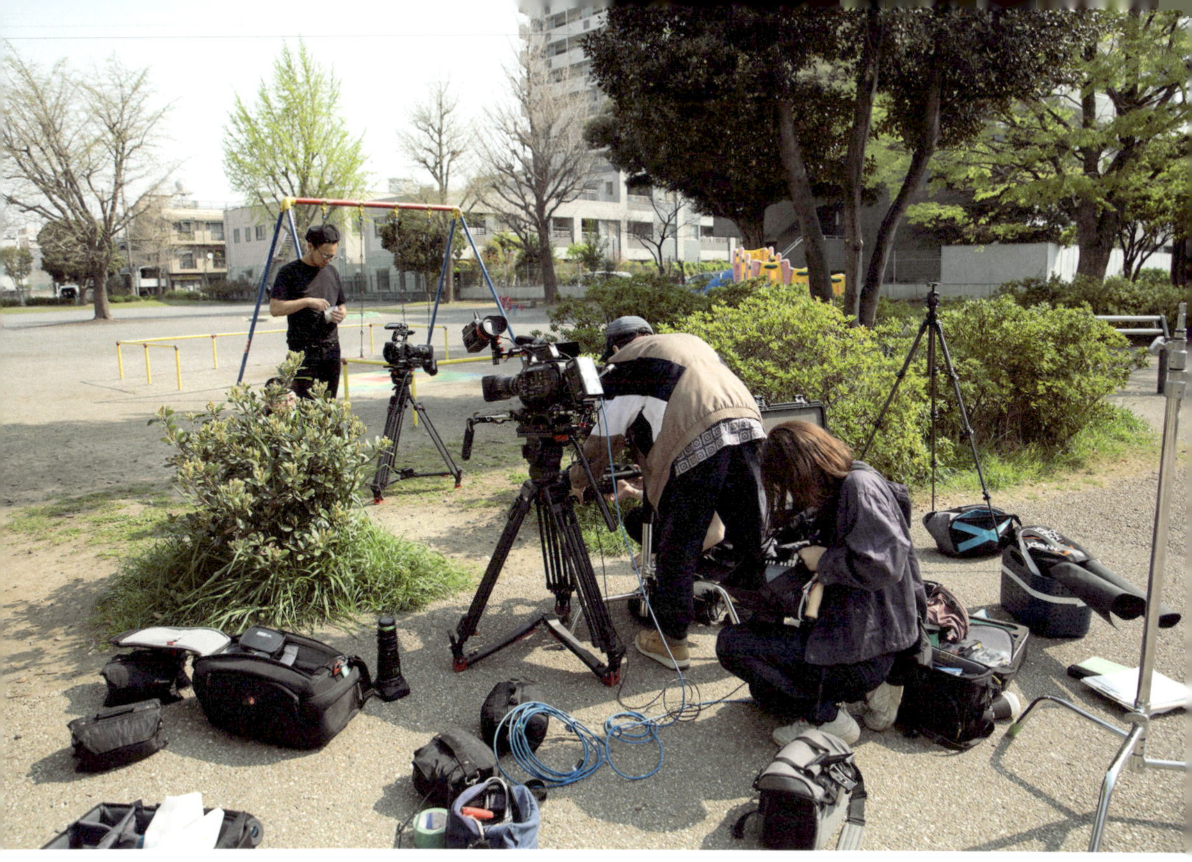

April 2, 2018

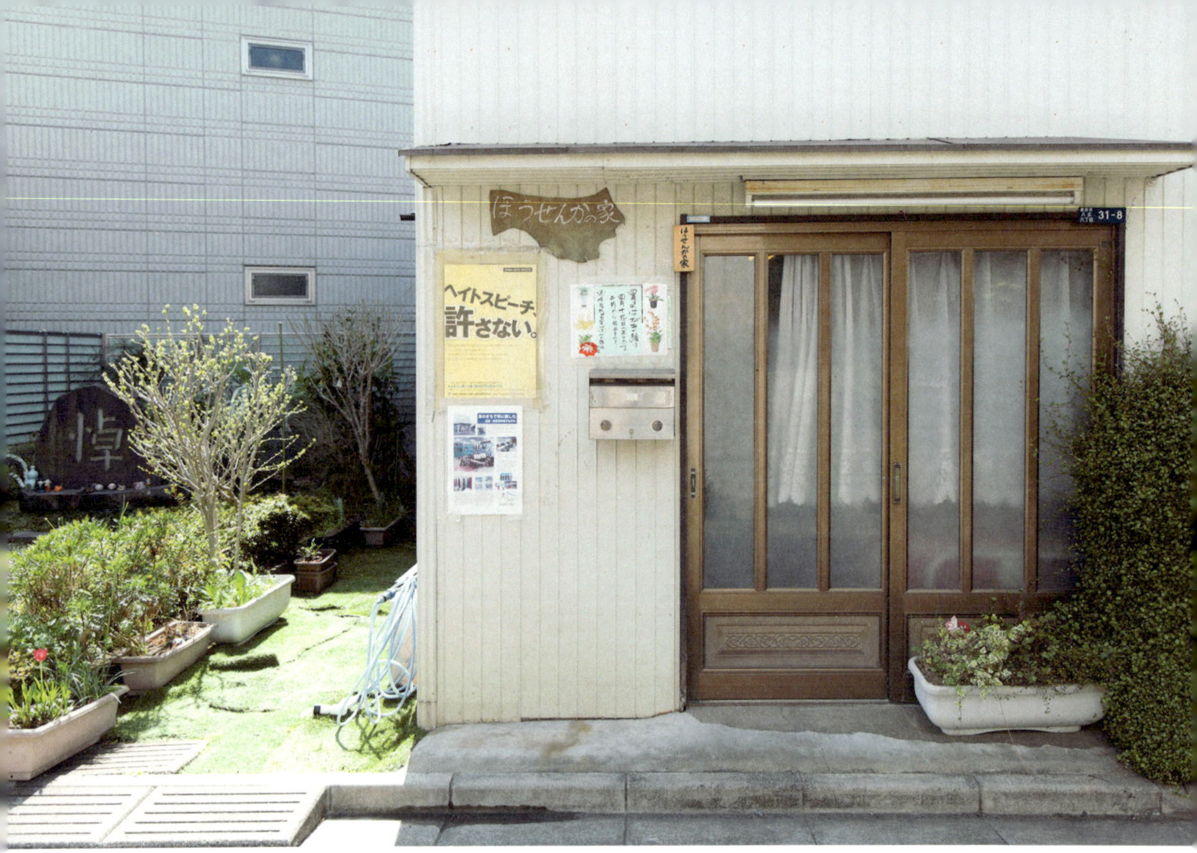

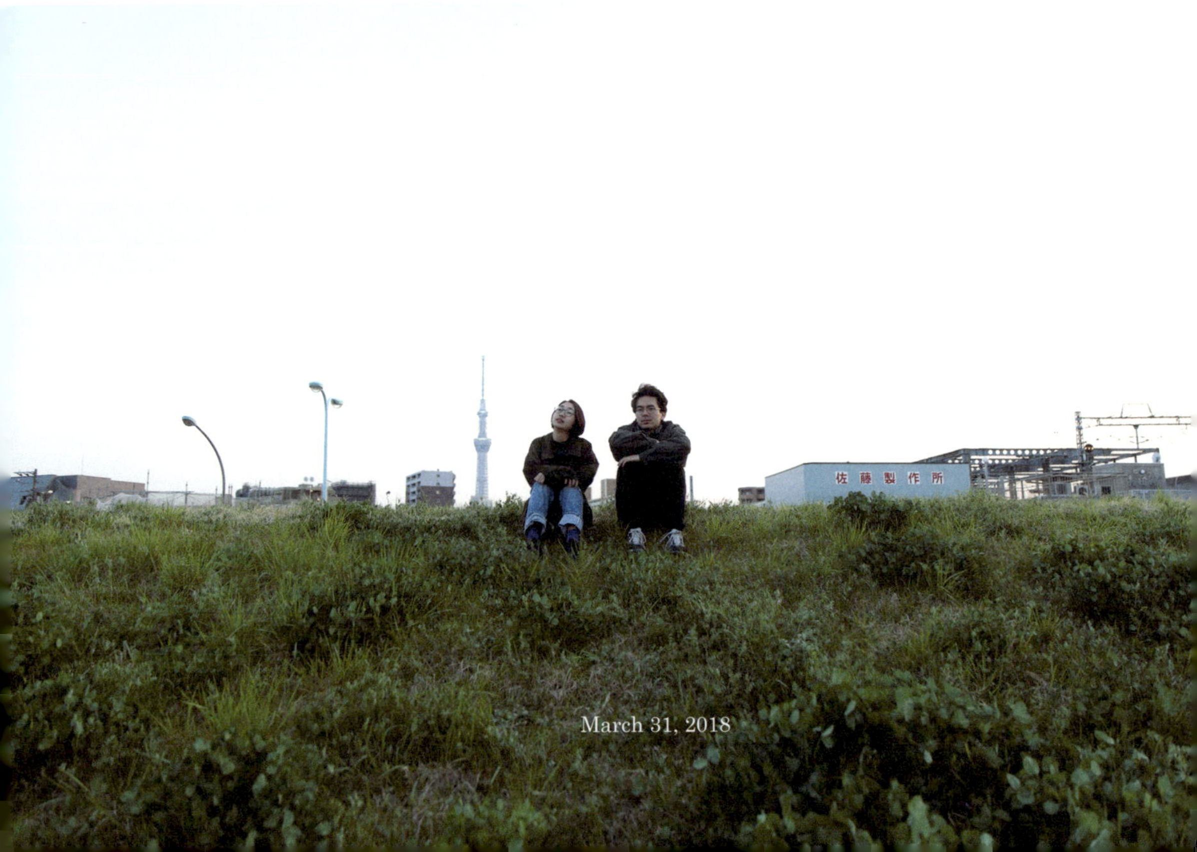

March 31, 2018

WOOHI CHUNG

Attended both "North" Korean and South Korean schools in Japan for six years each as *Zainichi* Korean. Studied at International Christian University since 2017. She is currently a graduate student at the same university and researching the memories of Korean Massacre after the Great Kantō earthquake in the field of Cultural Studies.

ELSA HIMMER

Studied art history with a focus on contemporary and medieval art at the University of Hamburg. Currently she is working at the Migros Museum für Gegenwartskunst in Zurich. Prior to this she worked as a student research assistant at the University of Hamburg, as a curatorial research assistant at the Bucerius Kunst Forum (Hamburg) as well as for the art mediation department of the Hamburger Kunsthalle. Her writings have appeared in a variety of publications and exhibition catalogues.

CHRISTIAN HOFER

Studied graphic design at the Fachklasse Grafik in Lucerne and continued his education as a designer from 2014 to 2017 at the Academy of Fine Arts in Leipzig. He lives in Basel and works as independent designer.

HEIKE MUNDER

Studied Cultural Studies at the University of Lunenburg. She has been the director of the Migros Museum für Gegenwartskunst in Zurich since 2001. She co-founded the Halle für Kunst Lüneburg e.V., which she co-directed between 1995 and 2001. Previously curated exhibitions include *Liz Magor* (2017), *Resistance Performed—Aesthetic Strategies under Repressive Regimes in Latin America* (2015), *Dorothy Iannone* (2014), *Geoffrey Farmer* (2013), *Ragnar Kjartansson* (2012), *Tatiana Trouvé* (2009), *It's Time for Action— There's No Option* (2006), *Marc Camille Chaimowicz* (2006), *Yoko Ono* (2005), and *Mark Leckey* (2003). She teaches regularly, including at the University of Lüneburg, Goldsmiths College (London), the University of Bern, the Zurich University of the Arts, and the Jan van Eyck Academy (Maastricht). Since 1995, she has written extensively on art in catalogues and art magazines. In 2012, she was on the jury of the Turner Prize.

TONG-HYON HAN

Is associate professor of sociology at the Japan Institute of the Moving Image. Born in Tokyo in 1968, she studied sociology at the Graduate School of Arts and Sciences of the University of Tokyo. Her research examines nationalism, the ethnicity of *Zainichi* Koreans in Japan, and relations between minority and majority groups. She is the author of *An Ethnography of the Chima-Chogori Uniform: Its Origin and Women's Agency at Korean Schools* (2006).

COLOPHON

This catalogue was published on the occasion of the exhibition *Koki Tanaka: Vulnerable Histories (A Road Movie)* at the Migros Museum für Gegenwartskunst, Zurich (August 25–November 11, 2018).

The exhibition was curated by Heike Munder.

PROJECT

Director / Artist
Koki Tanaka

Protagonists
Woohi Chung, Christian Hofer

Lecturer and Project Adviser
Tong-hyon Han

Lecturer
Masao Nishizaki (Housenka)

Legal Adviser
Takahiro Akedo

Lecturer for Preliminary Study Session
Tadahito Yamamoto (the Center of the Tokyo Raids and War Damage in Tokyo)

Director of Photography
Shinya Aoyama

Sound and Sound Editor
Ryota Fujiguchi

Lighting Design
Atsushi Sugimoto

Camera Operator
Yasuhiro Moriuchi

Production Manager
Saki Tanaka

Production Assistants
Natsuko Odate, Yoshiki Masuda

Camera Assistants
Miyazawa Hibiki, Natsumi Oikawa, Kana Nishio

Recording Assistant
Izuta Kadoaki

Coordination Assistant
    Yukino Sugaya

Drivers
    Hiroaki Yoshida, Shunsuke Takamizawa

Researcher
    Miwa Negoro

Cocktail Maker
    Atsushi Sugita

Background Cast Members
    Maki Hayashi, Chen Ay-Wen,
    Shihoka Imai, Yurika Kanda,
    Hitomi Kazama, Haruna Kobayashi,
    Takuya Misawa, Kaori Miyano,
    Ken Sasaki, Sakura Tokiyama,
    Yukinobu Watanabe, Wu Yin Feng,
    Hiroaki Yoshida

Filming Equipment Support
    ARTISTS' GUILD,
    RAKUDA STUDIO Co., Ltd.

Supported by
    Arts Council Tokyo (Tokyo Metropolitan
    Foundation for History and Culture)

ARTS
COUNCIL
TOKYO

Special thanks
    Naoki Kato

Fumio Inoue (CAMP),
Rika Fujiki (Mujinrto Production),
Hideki Aoyama (Aoyama Meguro)

Youngmi Lim, Andrew Maerkle

Keijiro Suga, Yoshitaka Mori,
Akihiro Kitada, Sunhe Cho,
Kyongfa Che, Kyung Hee Ha,
Maki Nishiyama, Mihoko Nishikawa,
Tomoko Yabumae,
Mami Suda (ARTISTS' GUILD),
Jin Kurashige (ARTISTS' GUILD),
Ryota Fujitsuka (Aoyama Meguro),
Nahoko Yamaguchi,
Kaoru Chiba (Arts Council Tokyo)

Arts Commons Tokyo,
Aoyama Meguro,
General Incorporated association:
Housenka,
Mujinrto Production,
Narita International Airport Corporation,
Vitamin Creative Space,
Yoshiko Isshiki Office

CATALOGUE

Published by Migros Museum für
Gegenwartskunst & JRP|Ringier

Editor
  Heike Munder

Managing Editor
  Dr. Raphael Gygax

Editorial Assistant / Image Editor
  Elsa Himmer

Translation from Japanese
  Andrew Maerkle

Translation from German
  Gerrit Jackson

Copyediting
  Anne O'Connor,
  Youngmi Lim (Tong-hyon Han)

Visual Concept & Graphic Design
  Studio Marie Lusa, Marie Lusa,
  Dominique Wyss

Lithography & Print
  Odermatt AG, Dallenwil

Photography
  Koki Tanaka
  (pp. 18, 21, 24–25, 31, 33–36, 39–42,
  44–45, 47–49, 52–54, 57, 60–64,
  67–68, 70–71, 98–99, 105, 113–114,
  121, endpaper),
  Woohi Chung's family albums
  (cover, pp. 12–15, 28 (bottom), 51,
  75–76, 104),
  Christian Hofer's family albums
  (pp. 28 (top), 80, 84–85, 88–89, 109,
  endpaper)

Printed in Switzerland

MIGROS MUSEUM FÜR GEGENWARTSKUNST

Director & Curator of the Exhibition
  Heike Munder

Curator
  Dr. Raphael Gygax

Head of Administration
  Catherine Reymond

Collection Curator
  Nadia Schneider Willen

Head of Press and Public Relations
  René Müller

Registrar / Scientific Researcher, Collection
  Franziska Bigger

Registrar / Scientific Researcher, Exhibitions
  Cornelia Huth

Head of Education and Public Programs
  Alena Nawrotzki

Art Educator
  Cynthia Gavranic

Administrative Assistant
  Stefanie Wolf

Intern
  Elsa Himmer

Head of Technical Services, Exhibitions
  Monika Schori

Technical Services, Exhibitions & Events
  Markus Bösch

Technical Services, Collection
  Marcel Meury

Coordinator Media Archive
  Gabi Deutsch

Coordinator Visitor Services
  Yuko Edelmann

Visitor Services
  Gregory Hari, Nico Meyer,
  Lena Mettler, Christa Michel,
  Valentina Minnig, Luzia Rink,
  Manuel Roman, Cynthia Schemidt,
  Yarin Shmerling, Raphael Stucky,
  Angela Walti

Technical Services
  Magdalena Baranya, Fabienne Bodmer,
  Christian Eberhard, Cristina Golland,
  Roman Gysin, Steffen Kuhn,
  Konstantinos Manolakis,
  Emanuel Masera, Wanda Nay,
  Tanja Roscic, Monika Stalder,
  Oli Wahmann

Migros Museum für Gegenwartskunst
Limmatstrasse 270
P. O. Box 1766
8031 Zurich
Switzerland
T +41 (0) 44 277 20 50
F +41 (0) 44 277 62 86
info@migrosmuseum.ch
migrosmuseum.ch

MIGROSMUSEUM
für Gegenwartskunst

An institution of the Migros Culture
Percentage.
migros-kulturprozent.ch

ISBN 978-3-03764-530-7

Distributed by

JRP|Ringier
Limmatstrasse 270
CH–8005 Zurich
T +41 (0) 43 311 27 50
E info@jrp-ringier.com
www.jrp-ringier.com

JRP|Ringier publications are available inter-
nationally at selected bookstores and from
the following distribution partners:

Switzerland
AVA Verlagsauslieferung AG,
Centralweg 16,
CH–8910 Affoltern a. A.,
avainfo@ava.ch, www.ava.ch

Germany and Austria
Vice Versa Distribution GmbH,
Potsdamer Str. 93,
D–10785 Berlin,
info@viceversaartbooks.com,
www.viceversaartbooks.com

France
Les presses du réel,
35 rue Colson,
F–21000 Dijon,
info@lespressesdureel.com,
www.lespressesdureel.com

UK and other European countries
Cornerhouse Publications, HOME,
2 Tony Wilson Place,
UK–Manchester M15 4FN,
publications@cornerhouse.org,
www.cornerhousepublications.org

USA, Canada, Asia, and Australia
ARTBOOK | D. A. P.,
75 Broad Street,
Suite 630,
US–New York, NY 10004,
orders@dapinc.com, www.artbook.com

For a list of our partner bookshops or for
any general questions, please contact
JRP|Ringier directly at info@jrp-ringier.com,
or visit our homepage www.jrp-ringier.com
for further information about our program.

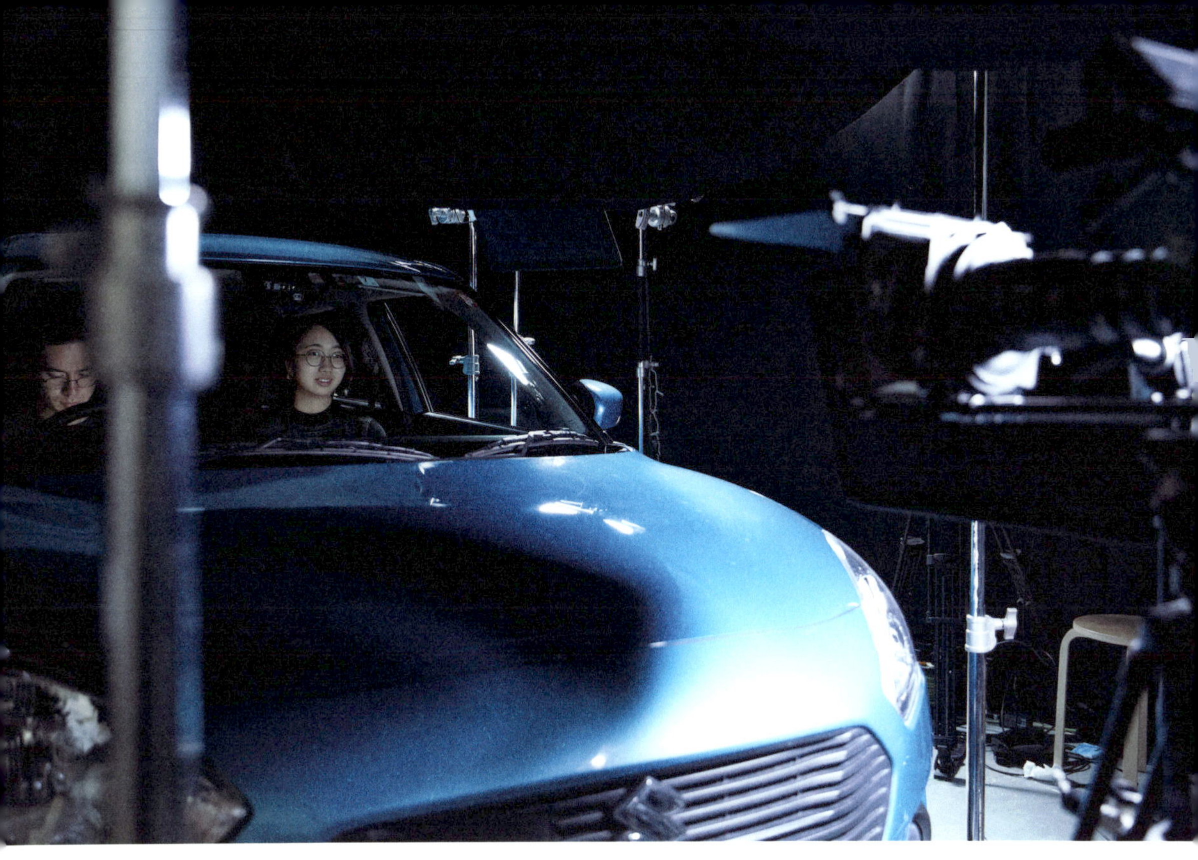

April 7, 2018

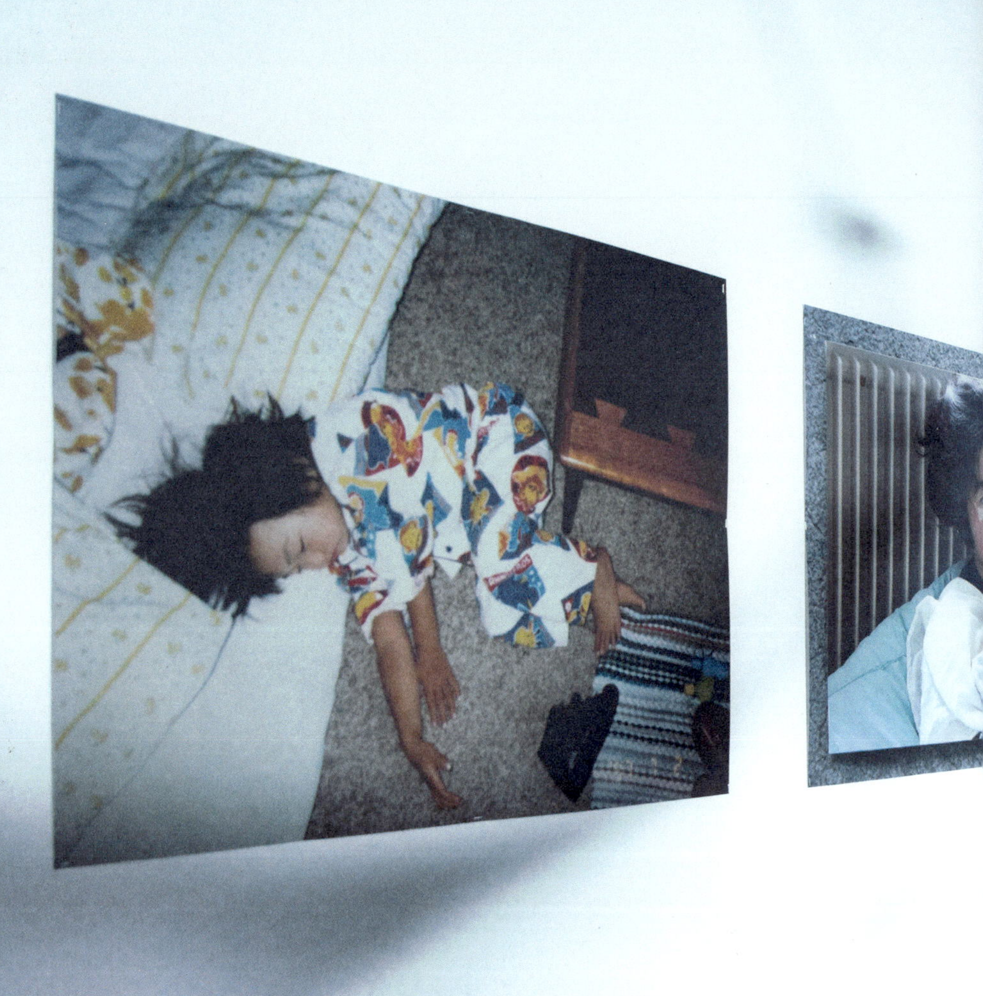